COMPASSIONATE MANAGEMENT

how ambitious creatives become kick-ass leaders

by Rena DeLevie

Copyright© 2017 Rena DeLevie

All rights reserved. No part of this book may be reproduced or transmitted in any form or by any means, electronic or mechanical, including photocopying, recording, or by any information storage and retrieval system, without permission in writing from the publisher. For information address: Management For Millennials.

Cover and book design: Anne Secor Art Direction & Design, www.annesecor.com
Fonts: Helvetica, Adobe Garamond Pro, Sacramento

ISBN-13: 978-1720318095
ISBN-10: 1720318093

This book is dedicated to Oren,
my favorite person in the entire universe,
who teaches me daily about
compassion, accountability, and love.

Dear Reader,

This book is written for people who want the world to be a better place. In my years as a leader and coach, I have worked with hundreds of people. Regardless of their generation, gender, sexuality, religion, ethnicity, and political beliefs, they all share one common desire: to be seen, heard, and understood. This book will resonate with people who are creative, strategic, business folk who are intense and empathetic. They're dedicated to doing great work that is fun and helps the planet. My kind of people.

That's why I wrote this book. It's a self-help/management book to guide each person to her own version of great management. There are 10 Innate Tools that each person uses to find her own management style. The core philosophy is compassion and accountability; how you choose to implement it is yours alone to decide.

Being a manager requires working closely with human beings and holding them accountable for delivering the goods. This can be scary for people who have been promoted due to their talent, yet given no management training. Does that sound familiar to you? That's most managers. That was me.

I was a graphic designer on the J.Crew catalog when the owner of J.Crew asked me to step into the role of manager. It was terrifying. It was an opportunity I jumped into and failed at repeatedly. Ask my peers whom I was suddenly managing. It was a disastrous few years where I followed the fear-based management culture and pushed away my friends who became direct reports. It took me years to realize what I was doing and what wasn't working. I had no models, no mentor, no guide to help me be my whole self and help others do the same. I squashed my empathetic nature and kept my intensity (bad idea); I rolled over people and ignored my gut saying something was off. I thought I was great. I mean Great! The work was getting done, things were more efficient because of my organizational skills, and I was getting paid a robust salary. So why wasn't I happy? And why would people run when I approached? Ok, that's a slight exaggeration. They would groan quietly.

I spent many years accepting being treated like poop and treating others the same; I thought it was a non-negotiable part of working and rising up the ladder. It was the norm. I had no exposure to anything different; all my friends had the same experience as me. When 9/11 happened, it shook me to the core and I began to shift. Who did I want to be in this world? What was I proud of in my long list of accomplishments? Was I happy managing the way I had been taught? I began to write notes of what didn't feel good and try the opposite. I began to show up fully as the sensitive, empathetic and intense person I am. The more I did this, the better I felt. And the more I was welcome into the work community.

And that's why this book exists. I want you to skip past the excruciatingly slow road I went down and zip straight to being the manager everyone wants to work for and with. That's a Compassionate Manager. The one who incorporates both compassion and accountability in every action, reaction and interaction. It's a management philosophy with core tenets that, when implemented, enable you to fully show up and lead with confidence. This book will open you up to a new way of thinking about management. It can be fun, meaningful, and lucrative. (Let's not underestimate the value of having a healthy salary.) Everyone has the potential for true managerial leadership, whether you're managing for the first time or have been for 10 years. Our style of day-to-day management evolves as we gain experience, but the foundation of compassion ensures a consistent and effective approach to bringing out the best in ourselves and in others.

I hope you find this helpful and fun,

Pava

Table of Contents

What is Compassionate Management   **15**

Compassionate Management Is Crucial   **25**

Innate Tools of Compassionate Management   **29**

    1. Be Your Self   30
    2. Trust Your Gut   31
    3. Own Your Power   32
    4. Benefit of the Doubt, Baby   33
    5. Not Taking It Personally   36
    6. Coexisting Truths   42
    7. Seen, Heard, and Understood   44
    8. Tone Of Voice   46
    9. Meet Your Inner Critic   48
    10. Be Self Aware   50

Essays   **53**

    Make Friends With Your Inner Critic   55
      • There She Goes Again   56
      • Anxiety About Anxiety Causes Anxiety   58
      • You Should Not Read This   60
      • Perfectionism Paralysis   62
      • The Comparer's Prison   63

    Setting Boundaries   67
      • Compassion Does Not Equal Doormat   68

Setting Boundaries (continued)	67
• Quiet Confidence Wins	70
• Turn A Personal Attack Into A Statement Of Fact	72
• Communication Style Matters	75
• The Mistreater's Journey	78
• Compassion Is NOT The Most Important Tool	80
• Post-Traumatic Job Disorder	83
Thriving During Difficult Times	87
• Embracing What Is	88
• Changing Our Thinking	90
• When To Share Gossip	93
• H.B.O.S.	95
• Buh-Bye Blame Game	97
Helping Ourselves	99
• Managing Up, Down, and Across	100
• Get Promoted	103
• Corporate Speak	106
• No One Can Succeed Alone	107
• With Each Age Come Gifts	109
• PDC Communication	111
Conclusion	**115**
Innate Tools Cheat Sheet (Rip this out and hang it in your office.)	**117**
About the Author	**119**

what is compassionate management

Compassionate Management is a management style where we apply compassion in place of fear. We do this internally; that's what makes it so powerful. It's not about trying to change anyone else; it's about shifting our own experience to make what could be a really difficult situation into a manageable one. Compassionate Management not only makes our lives more fun, it's also an antidote to Fear-Based Management.

In corporate America, most people only know the language of Fear-Based Management:

How to handle a frustrating moment? Yell.

How to deal with a difficult staff member? Threaten.

How to get the promotion? Push others out of the way.

Where did this begin? The culture of following a frighteningly forceful leader in order to survive is as old as time. It's deeply ingrained in our collective conscious, our corporate culture, and our everyday experiences. Think of the stories from the Bible, the dictators we've seen, and the stories on the news. It all comes down to a scary ruler who threatens our survival if we don't follow orders. Does this sound too dramatic for an office? I'll give you a few examples from my personal experience. You can't make this stuff up.

1. My boss told me to change the leading (space between lines of a sentence) to be tighter than our brand standards. I asked if he was sure and he demanded that I do it. When the final piece was published, he called me into his office and yelled at me for 2 hours, calling me a Nazi Communist for blindly following his orders. (I updated my resume that night.)

2. A copywriter fainted at the foot of our row of cubes. As he was lying on the floor, the senior manager stepped over him to point out a change she wanted in the layout. The designer, me, started to make the change, face frozen in fear. I finally unfroze and asked if the change could wait so we could help our friend on the floor. (The writer was fine after some orange juice.)

3. In a meeting of 45 people, an attendee questioned something the company owner strongly supported. I moved the conversation forward to limit attention to this topic. Later, I was reprimanded, "You should have shut her down. You should have publicly shamed her." (I had an out-of-body

experience during this interchange and left the company shortly thereafter.)

4. And one from a colleague—He was called in to Human Resources where he was told that he was fired because they had to let all VP's go. He said, "So I've just been promoted to VP?" And they said yes, he was. And unemployed as a result.

It's true that my career has been in the creative industry within the retail fashion sector, advertising, banking, insurance, and a touch of non-profit, but I've seen and heard about fear-based management experiences in every business sector. It's helpful to know if you've ever worked in a fear-based environment. If that sounds like a ridiculous statement, consider this. I once had a colleague pull me aside to whisper a question, 'did I feel anything in the office?' When I pressed her to be specific, she whispered, "Fear." It was plain as day to me as I had been working for many years, but it was her first job and she didn't have anything to compare it to. When I confirmed without hesitation, she made a sigh of relief at being validated. She thought she was crazy. I've had so many clients who felt that way. Fear-Based management can be subtle and insidious and hard to name. A quick way to determine if you've ever been managed with fear is to answer these questions:

1. Have you ever felt you'd be in trouble if you didn't do exactly as you were asked?
2. Is the office filled with sarcasm and sneakiness?

3. Is your tummy tight and are your teeth clenched all day?

If you answered yes, you've been diagnosed with fear-based management syndrome. (I just made that up.) It's everywhere, this fear-inducing style of management. The fact is, threats motivate people to do what is demanded. It's a short-term method to increase productivity or reduce cycle time. But in the long run, people will burn out in an environment like this. I did and so did my colleagues; we left behind the mediocre contributors who were fine with coasting.

It doesn't pay to churn and burn our employees. Fear closes us off from one another. It shuts down our primal need for connection. Fear creates a fight or flight reaction that results in an office of cave-people clubbing each other over the head. Let's quantify the loss created by fear-based management:

> Studies show that the cost to replace an employee is somewhere between 50-75% of that persons salary. Let's be conservative and say it's 50%. And let's be conservative and say that churn and burn companies lose only 10 employees a year at $70,000 per person. That's a loss of $350,000.00, in hard and soft cost of recruiting, interviewing, hiring, orientation and training, lost productivity, potential customer dissatisfaction, reduced or lost business, administrative costs, lost expertise and damage to our company's reputation. (We've all read a negative Glassdoor.com review and run as fast as we can.)

Churn and burn is an expensive assembly line of continued failure. All of which is avoidable. It just makes financial sense to treat people with compassion. I once had a boyfriend who told me, "I don't want to take care of anyone and I don't want anyone to take care of me." I ran out of that relationship at that moment. There was nowhere to go from there. It's the same at the office. If your employees feel and see that you don't care about their well-being, they'll go somewhere else or, even worse, they'll stay and do mediocre work. Compassion is universally and powerfully effective because it is a shared language that needs no explanation or training. It leads us to consider what someone else is experiencing and that enables us to partner more effectively and efficiently. Companies that implement compassion in their management approach have enormous success with productivity, creativity, and loyalty. Look at Trader Joe's, Zappos and Costco. Who doesn't like going to Trader Joe's? You watch the employees laugh together, help each other, and help customers with ease. That's trickle down Compassionate Management at work.

The internet has flattened the world in terms of opportunities and Millennials and GenZ's know they don't need to stay and put up with harsh management that doesn't nurture their innate talents and interests. Because of this freedom of choice, Millennials and GenZ's are shifting the dynamic at workplaces across the USA and the world by starting their own businesses or staying at jobs for 2 years before jumping to the next interesting adventure. This is different and scary for the folks who were building their careers before smart phones existed. Their fear has led to the entire generation being labeled cocky, bratty, and entitled. Sure there are a few Millennials who fit this description, but I promise you that there were a few cocky twenty-somethings in every generation before and will be after.

I say let's stop blaming Millennials for the changes happening around us. Let's build bridges to learn from each other and make good money in the process. Compassionate Management is the management technique that connects people beyond generation and level of experience. Compassion levels the field regardless of age, culture, gender, sexuality, function, tenure, title, or economic status. Add religion, location, and any other diversity stats you want. Compassion is universally and powerfully effective. A Compassionate Manager is someone who advocates for the team, who creates a safe space for creativity, partnership, and trust, and who holds everyone, including herself, accountable to deliver actions that will benefit the company, the team and her Self. Compassionate Management is giving yourself, and others, permission to be angry and kind and pissed off and understanding all at once, and to communicate all of that appropriately. When we do this, we can shift our culture to one of mutual accountability and collaboration.

Mindfulness is the underlying thread of Compassionate Management. It's about awareness of self and others. General Mills, Intel, Target, Mayo Clinic, United Way, and the World Economic Forum in Davos are a few of the many organizations investing in mindfulness trainings. Just like with Compassionate Management, these mindfulness approaches result in associates who shift from frustration to positivity, who manage their emotions with professionalism and self-awareness, and who successfully collaborate with each other. There are hundreds of mindfulness apps, and endless books to read on the subject of mindfulness approaches to healthy and balanced living. Emotional Intelligence, by Daniel Goleman, was on The New York Times bestseller list for a year-and-a-half with more than 5,000,000 copies in print worldwide in 30 languages. Denis Hay, an anger management specialist who teaches Compassion Workshops in Australia, published these results:

35% improvement in self-esteem
250% increase in strategies to resolve anger
33% clinical anxiety reduced to normal level

That's some impressive statistics! I've been practicing Mindfulness and mindfulness meditation for 14 years and I know the value of awareness. I've sat in sessions where we try to quiet our mind so as to give us the ability to be calm in this hectic world. There is enormous value in opening up to these mindful methodologies. The intention of Compassionate Management is to connect the mindfulness mindset with the realities of everyday corporate America.

First we start with identifying the 10 Innate Tools that exist within each of us. They're like muscles we didn't know we had until we're forced to use them. Rather than wait until you have to move something heavy, start building your core up now. In other words, everything else works better when our Compassionate Management muscles are engaged.

The 10 Innate Tools of Compassionate Management are:

1. Be Your Self - When we show up fully and quietly confident
2. Trust Your Gut - When we trust our deepest knowing
3. Own Your Power - When we control how we respond
4. BOD, Baby - Giving others the Benefit of the Doubt
5. Not Taking It Personally - When we decide it's not about us
6. Coexisting Truths - Opposing truths do not negate each other
7. Seen, Heard, and Understood - The universal desire
8. Tone Of Voice - Meaning changes as our intonation changes
9. Meet Your Inner Critic - Disarm the internal terrorist
10. Be Self Aware - We choose who we want to be in this world

As you scanned this list, did any call out to you? For example, did you suddenly realize that you almost never give someone the benefit of the doubt? This is your opportunity to consider why that is, and with whom. Is it with certain people or everyone? And now that you're aware of it, can you begin shifting it? Go to page 33 right now to read in detail about BOD, Baby. You'll learn about the what, how and why of giving people the benefit of the doubt. Section 3 of this book is where I describe the what, how and why of each of these 10 Innate Tools. Every reader of this book owns every one of these tools; you just may not know it yet. The purpose of this book is to guide you to access these innate tools to have the most fulfilling career (and life) possible. I know that's a tall order, but I've seen it happen over and over.

Skip sections if you want, or turn the page and immerse yourself in the essays where I show these tools in action. There's no one-way to read this book. Like Compassionate Management itself, the content is here for you to internalize and implement however you choose. Read on.

compassionate management is crucial

In the 30 years I've worked in the corporate sector, I have rarely seen management be consistently respectful towards others, treat people of different levels as equals, or show compassion towards themselves or others. Instead, I've seen management practice what I call Fear-Based Management, where secrecy, favoritism, and threat of job loss are the norm. Changing this is what drives me.

I have seen and worked with so many people who have been beaten down psychologically and can't see their own gifts. I was one of these people. That's why I help people learn to see themselves with compassion and recognize their gifts and eliminate the need for validation from others. People who find out they're awesome (we're all awesome at something!) immediately start delivering at a higher level because they're no longer weighed down by fear, insecurity, or resentment.

People manage with fear when that's all they've experienced and witnessed, and they see the Fear-Based Management being rewarded with promotions and corner offices. The prevalence of Fear-Based Management means that few people have a comfort level with being kind, respectful, and communicative. They're only comfortable with the familiar experience of fear, insecurity and resentment. This leads to an office filled with barriers to communication and little to no trust. This lack of trust and communication is like a dam in the river of information and creativity. There is a concrete wall blocking true connection.

We must know the truth of what our associates at every level are experiencing in order to ensure the most efficient, effective, productive, and creative environment. We must address this immediately and continually. It's crucial to the health of an organization. Each brand needs a healthy dynamic allowing the members at every level to collaborate, cheer each other on, cover for each other as needed, and partner respectfully.

Fear-Based Management is a disease that is being eliminated from the inside out by courageous people bringing their whole gorgeous selves to the office, one person at a time.

This isn't a kumbaya group hug; this is an effective and proven method to develop self-awareness, compassion, and accountability in the workplace, which leads directly to respect, kindness, and communication. This works at every level of seniority. No one is too young or old for this transformation.

No one is too senior or too junior either. It can start at any level and is bound to spread like luscious wild fire. Just like fear - compassion, kindness, and collaboration spread quickly when implemented consistently.

What drives me? I have witnessed and experienced the power of compassion as a business tool, balanced with accountability. It's quite a heady mix that leaves me feeling tipsy with hope for a delicious corporate America like we've never seen before.

innate tools of compassionate management

Human beings are born with a toolbox of coping mechanisms and intuition; yet most of us never pay attention to these tools. We all know how to breathe, yet we rarely give breathing a thought. The tools you're about to dive into are as innate and natural as breathing. These tools are inside you right now. Allow yourself to read, reflect, and then implement these innate tools of Compassionate Management.

The fastest way to start using the tools is to pay attention to the feeling in your body as you read about a tool. That feeling becomes a "flag," a way for you to connect your emotional and physical responses to a situation. This "flag" enables you to quickly identify which tool to use in the heat of the moment. After a few instances of noting the flags, it becomes second nature because what you're really doing is calling upon your deepest knowing. It doesn't feel like work then; it feels natural, easeful, and powerful.

1. BE YOUR SELF

They chose you. Show up. Fully. There is no one else like you and they asked You to join the team.

It's when we show up fully, and quietly confident, that we truly feel comfortable, and others sense that. People want to be around people who are comfortable with themselves.

When you interviewed, you tried to knock their socks off by showing what a powerhouse you were. Maybe now that you're there, it feels scary because you want to fit in. But fitting in never really works.

There are so many labels we use to pigeonhole people as a way to feel okay with how [insert your label] we are. Be your quirky, silly, normal, serious, artsy, nerdy, intellectual, airy fairy, self. Wear your label proudly and go forth and deliver your best work. It will inspire your colleagues to do the same.

The more we fully show up, the more we are seen as leaders: courageous souls who model being themselves and make it safe for others to follow suit.

Be Your Self. The more we fully show up as our quirky, silly, normal, or serious selves, the more we are seen as Leaders.

2. TRUST YOUR GUT

Trust your gut; the body doesn't lie. This powerful statement can help you in every area of your life.

Your heart is feelings; your head is facts. Your gut takes both pieces of information, churns them up, and spits out the answer. It's called instinct and everyone has it. The challenge is developing the ability to hear the gut over the other two loud voices of head and heart.

How to describe the gut speaking to you? It's physically located in your belly, right above your navel. It can be a fight or flight feeling or a slow "ugh" coming on or a fluttery "this is fantastic" or "I want to try it!" or so many other possibilities. There may be just an awarenes of something un-name-able.

You can choose to ignore the butterfly in your tummy or you can hone your ability to listen to her. She's talking to you. Remember, the gut gathers data from the head and feeling from the heart and spits out a solution. Often it's not an obvious solution or even one you want. But it is the right solution. Think of your gut as your muse. The voice from above that guides you. Except she's in you.

Once you're truly tuned in, there will be no question of which action or inaction to take.

Trust Your Gut. It combines feelings and facts to deliver the right solution.

3. OWN YOUR POWER

True power is how we treat ourselves and how we treat others. Everyone has power. Some people appear to have more power in a company than others, but the truth is we all have power over how we react to a person, place, or thing.

The fact is, the reaction is more important than the thing. Do I yell, or breathe and ask more questions? Do I slam the door, or walk out diplomatically? Do I quit on the spot, or take some time to consider my options? Do I refuse to lay off 20% of the team and get fired myself, or do I lay them off compassionately?

The way we respond is the way we Own Our Power. If we let others dictate how we handle a situation, we are giving away our power.

Don't skim past this tool. Owning your power is paramount. It is the nectar of life and the secret password to satisfaction in your work. Your power is yours to keep forever. It was offered to you as you arrived in this life form and the offer still stands today. You can disregard the offer and keep handing your power to unworthy people, or you can embrace your divine power and use it wisely, with compassion for yourself, and others. In that order.

Own your power and use it wisely.

How we react is how we Own Our Power. If we let others dictate how we handle a situation, we are giving away our power.

4. BENEFIT OF THE DOUBT, BABY

Benefit of the Doubt is the practice of deciding to believe someone, even if you're not sure that what the person is saying is true. Why? Because it feels good. It sounds obvious, but it's amazing how easy it is for people to assume the worst and stay in a place of anger and negativity. Fear sends us directly to fight or flight, and when we can't flee, we fight. We make assumptions of guilt about our colleagues without even realizing it. If you've ever felt wrongly accused of something, you're likely a recipient of this assumption of guilt. And how often have you grumbled some snarky comment about someone being late to your meeting only to find out that he was late for a valid reason? We've all done this. It's human, but it's not a fun way to live. And it's a choice. For real.

Giving others the benefit of the doubt allows us to see the best in our colleagues, which frees us from the negative associations we subconsciously ascribe to people. This creates an environment for positive and mutually beneficial work relationships.

Choose to give someone the Benefit of the Doubt and see how it goes for you. Chances are you'll feel good about it. I don't mean let down your guard and allow someone to step all over you. I mean consider each situation and see if you can allow yourself to give someone the BOD, Baby.

Assumption of Guilt (what I call AOG) is outward facing;

Benefit of the Doubt (what I call BOD) is inward facing. People who choose Assumption of Guilt are often afraid to look inward, to hold themselves accountable. It feels safer to quickly blame others for being late to a meeting rather than consider that we may not have set up the meeting to be at an appropriate time, have a clear agenda, or a compelling benefit to those whom we've invited.

To look inward and assess what went wrong with the meeting is to hold ourselves accountable for creating a meeting worth coming to. It's a sharing of responsibility. This thinking applies to meetings, yes, but also to how we treat each other on a daily basis, whether you report to me or I report to you.

Here's the other incredibly neat thing about Benefit of the Doubt. It's infectious. When you embrace it and practice it consistently, others will also. And when that starts to happen, it's magic! Like a stone in a lake, Benefit of the Doubt ripples quickly. A lot faster than Assumption of Guilt actually. It makes sense – Assumption of Guilt is dense, heavy, and sad. Benefit of the Doubt is light, bouncy and fun.

Practice Benefit of the Doubt outside of work first. Choose to give that driver who cut you off the benefit of the doubt. He had to pee really badly, she was in labor, or they were catching a flight. It doesn't make their unsafe driving okay. It makes your experience of their unsafe driving a benign distraction, or an exercise in creativity. It might even make you giggle when you realize how much energy you had been investing in silly little, meaningless anger.

I like to call it "BOD, Baby" because the phrase is fun, easy to remember, and the alliteration is catchy. This is important because you're going to want others to join you in this effort and more people will listen if they're having fun. When I've been accused of something inaccurate, I say, "Hey, give me the benefit of the doubt. Remember BOD, baby!" It usually dissipates tension in the room and we can laugh and shift to collaboration instead of fear.

Giving others the Benefit Of The Doubt frees us from the negative associations we subconsciously ascribe to people.

5. NOT TAKING IT PERSONALLY

BOD, Baby leads us right here to Not Taking It Personally. Truly the most freeing choice we can make is to not take it personally. It's making the shift from negative thought to neutral thoughts. This is by far one of the hardest things for humans to accomplish on a regular basis. But it's a choice and, once we realize this, we can choose a happier path.

Taking things personally is either:

1. Accepting someone's accusation as our truth

2. Creating a story where it's possible none exists

When I ask an audience how many times they've done either 1 or 2, all hands go up. We've all done this, which means we have all given away our power. And when we give away our power, we end up suffering. We experience the pain of helplessness, insecurity, and lack of confidence.

There is zero benefit to taking it personally, whereas Not Taking It Personally is freeing, empowering and energizing. Like all effective methodologies, it takes root when we practice it repeatedly. Here's the formula for Not Taking It Personally:

Step #1. Recognize when we're taking it personally

Step #2. Define the meaning we are applying

Step #3. Factualize it

Step #4. Move forward

Let's dig a little deeper in the most crucial and hardest step.

Step #1. Recognize when we're taking it personally.

The goal is to develop self-awareness of something we've accepted as the norm for many years. It starts with real-time awareness of how our bodies react to someone. Did my heart race when he said that, or did I clench my fists when I read that email, or why do I always grit my teeth around her?

Now we'll do an exercise to help you recognize how your body reacts to a trigger.

"With all due respect…"

Stop and analyze what reactions your body had when you read that phrase. Do these resonate?

Jaw clenched	Heart raced
Tummy tightened	Fists gripped
Face flushed	Breathing shortened
Eyes squinted	Chest constricted

What else would you add?

Each body reacts uniquely. It's important to know what our individual body does as this is our personal map guiding us to decipher what's happening around us. And when we can consistently recognize a body reaction, we can then teach ourselves to Pause. Until then, we are trigger-responsive and that usually results in counter-productive feelings and behavior.

Paying attention to what our bodies are doing is a direct short cut to awareness of what our minds are thinking. Our body says, "Attack in progress!" and our mind instinctively agrees. So now we "know" we've been attacked personally. But have we? And that's where the Pause is a gift to ourselves, allowing us a moment to consider how we want to respond.

> *A Common Trigger:*
> Tone of Voice (Innate Tool #8) is relevant here. Tone of voice is the primary communicator in a conversation; the actual sentence content is not. Therefore, Tone Of Voice is likely the main trigger that sends us into Taking It Personally. Awareness of tone is another short cut to Not Taking It personally.

Let's look at 3 different scenarios where most humans end up feeling personally attacked, and how we can choose to Not Take It Personally by using the formula and by making mind shifts.

WHEN IT REALLY ISN'T PERSONAL

"Why was the ABC project late?"

Step #1. Recognize when we're taking it personally

I did NOT delay the project! There were many factors contributing to the missed deadline! I worked really hard… WAIT! I'm receiving that question as a personal attack.

Step #2. Define the meaning we are applying

I'm interpreting that statement as an accusation that I caused the delay. I didn't, but I do feel uncomfortable about the project being delivered late.

Step #3. Factualize it

I began working on the project the minute I received the information. The information came 6 days late. And then the reviews happened 4 days late. It was a cascade of missed deadlines along the way.

Step #4. Move forward

"The project was late as there was a cascade of missed deadlines along the way due to the circuitous lifecycle we have right now. We're streamlining processes as we speak to ensure this doesn't happen again."

WHEN IT MIGHT ACTUALLY BE PERSONAL

"I didn't realize you were invited to this meeting."

Step #1. Recognize when we're taking it personally

Of course I'm invited! Does he think I'm not bringing value here! What a jerk… WAIT! I'm taking this statement personally.

Step #2. Define the meaning we are applying

I'm interpreting that statement as an accusation that I forced my way in or that I'm in competition with him.

Step #3. Factualize it

I was invited. I guess the organizer values my contribution. I have nothing to feel uncomfortable about. I assumed he would be invited because of his role in the project. He must be in competition with me. His snarkiness is about his own insecurity; it has nothing to do with me.

Step #4. Move forward

"I was invited. It's an exciting project."

There's a third scenario to consider that happens in the workplace much more regularly. The real-time thought shift to help us through a difficult experience. Let's take a look:

You're running a meeting. You look around the table and see:

Sideways glances. Choose your thought:

He is glancing sideways at her because they both think that you are clueless.

He's glancing sideways at her because they're having an affair.

Yawns. Choose your thought:

She's yawning because you run a horribly boring meeting.

She's yawning because her puppy was demanding attention at 4am.

Grimaces. Choose your thought:

He's grimacing because you keep suggesting bad ideas.

He's grimacing because he ate something funny at lunch.

This doesn't mean you can skip out on running a great meeting. We still can learn from grimaces and yawns, but in the moment of running the meeting, we cannot allow distractions to take us off point. That's why shifting from negative to neutral thoughts are effective.

The fact is, a statement has no emotional meaning until we apply meaning. When we choose to Not Take It Personally, we have the power to assign any meaning we want, including one that isn't personal.

We may still get annoyed, angry, or frustrated because someone behaved inappropriately, but we have freed ourselves from unnecessary drama and enabled ourselves to focus on what's important.

Not Taking It Personally frees us from the impact of others' drama and puts us in the seat of Power.

6. COEXISTING TRUTHS

Work is much easier to handle when we name the many factors contributing to our joy and frustration. Allow yourself to name the annoying and the fun. The silly and the exasperating. Let's pretend you have been promoted and you have new responsibilities; it's so exciting! And scary. That's a coexisting truth.

It's rare that we're taught to honor multiple emotions simultaneously. This means we often are left with just squealing about how excited we are to be promoted. This leaves no room for asking for support, and we hide in our cubicle thinking about how scared we are and afraid to tell anyone lest they think we're not excited.

There is a belief that one truth negates the other. This is not true! We are capable of feeling many conflicting emotions at once; all have validity and need to be acknowledged.

Most work experiences are both: exciting AND scary, demanding AND satisfying, or silly AND exasperating. When we allow ourselves to name this dual truth, we can identify the kind of support we need with confidence. This is a wonderful gift we can give ourselves. Holistic clarity of our experience, and a clear sense of what we need to succeed.

When we then take this quiet, internally recognized coexisting truth and share it with our manager and/or direct reports, we accomplish three things.

1. We make it safe for others to state their dual truths. We model the compassion we show towards ourselves and we ask for what we need with clarity.

2. We can hold our manager and direct reports accountable to help us. They aren't mind readers; they trust us to do our job well or ask for help. Once you state your coexisting truths, they become accountable to help you.

3. We can hold our manager and direct reports accountable to share with us when they have coexisting truths. (This eliminates surprises! I love this!)

The action of coexisting truths is to treat oneself with compassion and accountability, and ask others to do the same. Now that's Compassionate Management.

Coexisting Truths allow us to feel the whole experience; the good, bad, ugly, and delightful.

7. SEEN, HEARD, AND UNDERSTOOD

This is the basis of most suffering in the workplace (and the world). People want to be seen, heard, and understood. More powerful than being "yes'd" all day long, they want to have a consistently valued voice. Quality people want truth. If their ideas don't meet the objectives, they want to understand and have it explained with kindness.

To clarify - we're not talking about looking deeply into a direct reports eyes and saying; "I want to know you truly, deeply, madly." We're talking about committing to seeing each person as an individual with unique talents, skills, and interests. So often people feel like cogs in the wheel or assembly line employees. It's demotivating to feel this way and doesn't benefit the company to have this management approach because people will leave; they'll find a different job where they feel valued.

But first they'll stick around and be miserable. This is where low morale starts. Those folks who feel undervalued, taken for granted, and underutilized. It's up to us to make sure this doesn't happen or, if it's already happened, to turn it around.

We can say we're committed to this with words and phrases and posters, but we all know it's the actions that speak the loudest. Here's what Seen, Heard, and Understood looks like:

> Rebecca wants a promotion, but leadership knows Rebecca's not ready. The areas in which she needs to evolve are com-

municated with compassion, clarity, and accountability. She doesn't have to wonder why she didn't get promoted, or how to get there. Now she has a clearly defined path.

Jenny has a personal connection to the non-profit aligned with the company. When it's time to do that pro bono project, she gets to lead it. Everyone benefits- she'll bring her all to it, which makes the company look great, and she'll gain confidence and broaden her visibility company-wide.

Brandon has communicated that he needs a private office in order to deliver the level of work being asked of him, but the company protocol is cubicles for all but executives. Brandon witnesses his manager advocate on his behalf and is excited. It would be fantastic to get the office, but whether he gets it or not, he feels Seen, Heard, and Understood by his direct manager. He may leave the company anyway because he doesn't like cubicles, but we can't control that. We can only control how we treat Brandon.

It is the responsibility of leadership to ensure that we nurture this mindset; that it becomes the default way our teams partner. Without a leader who truly listens to us, we are left hanging out to dry. Make the commitment to pause and try to really "see" every member of the team, no matter their level, tenure, or track record. It will come back to you in spades.

Being Seen, Heard, and Understood is a universal desire that crosses cultures, gender, industries, and generations.

8. TONE OF VOICE

Did you ever hear yourself say something and think, "Did I just use an inappropriate tone of voice?" Me neither. I usually get that hot flash, cold sweat of realization when I'm called on it or when I hear my kid copy me. (Wow, that gets my attention.) Usually I'm in a conversation and the pressure is building and in a flash I lower my standards "just to get through the moment." I excuse poor behavior because I'm thinking 5 steps ahead instead of being present in the moment.

Let's look at examples of Tone of Voice from annoying to cruel:
Nice shirt. (condescending)
Nice shirt. (genuine)

Is the report done? (condescending)
Is the report done? (genuine)

Why did you do that? (condescending)
Why did you do that? (genuine)

Notice how the intensity of meaning increases with the examples. There are implied statements in all cases, but the last one cuts the deepest. It's clear the condescending person has already decided why you did that and that your reasons were idiotic. You've just been called an idiot. There's no room for conversation, which means there's no opportunity for building trust and understanding. This eliminates the possibility for partnership, which leaves the organization in silos. Like those lonely towers filled with corn on the plains of Iowa.

My intention is to be a cool cucumber at all times and never use a snotty, condescending, or patronizing tone of voice. I can hear you all laughing because it's just not possible to be a robot if you're a human being. We're lucky to be human. Our emotions are gifts to be managed with compassion and commitment. I'd even got so far as to say it's our responsibility, (for peace on earth!) to manage our emotions with compassion and commitment.

All it takes is to think before you talk. It's one of the hardest commitments to maintain and when you have compassion for how hard it is, it becomes easier to maintain. (Say that 10 times fast.) Seriously, compassion for the challenge makes the challenge easier.

Tone of voice makes a huge difference in communication at work, at home, at the grocery store. Wherever you communicate, bring compassion to your commitment to think before you speak. The response will be worth it.

Tone Of Voice is the music we use to relate to each other. The quality of answers is dependent on the tone of questions.

9. MEET YOUR INNER CRITIC

Your main source of anxiety, your internal terrorist, have you met this creature? You know, the voice that berates you all day and night. The one who keeps telling you you're too this and too that and not this enough and not that enough.

Trying to negotiate with that inner critic- the voice who says you're not capable or smart enough or whatever- is a waste of your energy. That inner critic is loud and stubborn and only wants to tear you down. It's like trying to negotiate with a terrorist.

Better to use your energy to recognize that the inner critic is gabbing again and that you're going to let her, while knowing in your heart that you are capable and even if you fall on your face, you'll get up and keep going.

Another way to think about it is this: Who is listening to that inner critic? You. The real You. I'm not saying you're schizophrenic and hearing voices; I'm saying, we all have a true Self who can listen to the nagging voice saying "you're too this and too that and if only you did this..." and if you can listen to her you can also discredit her.

The way to do this is to get to know your inner critic. Say hi to her and invite her to the table. Recognize that if you can talk to her, she isn't YOU. Your Inner Critic will keep jammering on; it's her job and she is desperate to keep it. You can feel compassion for her, so terrified of losing her job. And then you can allow her to keep her job and just ignore her. Now you can laugh and breathe and not give her credibility anymore. Maybe even identify whose voice it is. Oh that's my teacher, oh that's my relative, oh that's my… That's not ME, so it's not meaningful.

It's simply noise.

Learning to differentiate your true Self from your inner critic is not as hard as it sounds. It's a matter of listening and realizing that you're listening. Learning to tune her out rather than expecting her to stop is the big challenge.

Meeting Your Inner Critic enables you to disarm this inner terrorist.

10. BE SELF AWARE

Who do I want to be in this world? This is the metric against which to measure how we handle a situation. Whether there is an ethical question about budget management, or a performance assessment to be made about a direct report – we can use this question as a barometer to ensure we maintain integrity at work every day.

There are internal flags to help us Be Self Aware.

Pay attention to what we're basing decisions on. Am I fighting my boss because she reminds me of my old art teacher who tormented me? (I did this quite a bit before I realized it.)

Consider how our actions affect others. When I yelled at her, did everyone cringe and slink away to avoid me for the rest of the day? (Ouch. This one stings.)

Consider how others reactions affect us. Did I get that sinking feeling when they were laughing at my idea? (I did. I still do.)

Now we need to take the information gathered and get quiet. We need to look inside to figure out why we're affected the way we are in each of these scenarios.

These steps happen all day long and it becomes a natural part of our lives to self-monitor in a loving way. "Hey, I have that sinking feeling again, why? Ah, I need to revisit that conversation with her and find a fair resolution."

Self-awareness ties directly into Owning Our Power. The more self-aware we are, the more we can decide how we want to handle a situation and be able to look ourselves in the mirror each day. Compassionate self-awareness and self-accountability are the qualities of true leadership.

Be Self Aware of who you want to be in this world and let that drive your every action and reaction.

Essays

make friends with your inner critic

Your inner critic is the person talking to you all day and night. She lives inside and she berates, makes fun of, taunts, and torments you with her critical words and thoughts.
But if she's talking and you're listening, then she's not You. And you can disarm her. It's an amazing gift to yourself. Read on.

There She Goes Again

Have you met your Inner Critic? You know, the voice that berates you all day and night. The one who keeps telling you you're too this and too that and not this enough and not that enough. Consider this: if you can hear her talking, who is talking and who is listening?

Ah yes, my wise colleague. 'Tis you listening to your IC as she jabbers on and on demanding your attention. IC's love attention. It feeds them and keeps them active and energetic. Attention to IC's is like oxygen to us humans.

Chances are, you react to your IC in one of three typical ways: Fight with her to convince her she's wrong, agree and beat yourself up, or try your darndest to ignore her.

The trick to disarming your inner critic is to acknowledge her. Not agree, disagree, or debate. Simply acknowledge.

An example:

You've just had a business lunch and on the way out, while you're schmoozing the client, your IC is telling you that you "shouldn't have eaten that fettuccine. It's loaded with gluten and carbs and it's going straight to your thighs. And by the way, your skirt is tight enough on your thighs, thank you very much."

Do you:

Tell her your skirt is tight because it just came out of the dryer, darn it!

Tell her she's right. You're a loser.

Speak louder to your client until he starts looking at you funny (because you're trying to drown out your IC).

Instead, try this: "Oh, there she goes again."

It's a simple acknowledgment of the fact that your IC is blabbing again. It is NOT recognition of WHAT she's blabbering about. The content of her blabbering is fluff. It's icky, bad for you, medicinal-tasting cotton candy. There's no need to consider the content at all. At all. Merely stating "Oh, there she goes again" in a calm and neutral voice is the key to disarming this internal terrorist. It's a calm way of communicating "I hear ya but you've got no power over me. I know you're just a sad and lonely critic; you're not Me."

Try it out with any IC commentary:

You're such a slow runner; everyone else will get there before you. "There she goes again."

You're so worried about how your hair will look in this humidity. God, you're vain. "There she goes again."

You didn't get that promotion because you're not smart enough. "There she goes again."

As her critiques escalate, your response stays neutral and disarming. I swear it disarms her. It takes practice and commitment to stay neutral and disengaged from her commentary; the rewards are priceless. It becomes muscle memory to simply acknowledge and move forward with whatever it is you're doing.

Suddenly your background theme changes from criticism to "Go for Greatness!" This is another neutral statement that doesn't mean you're not terrified or excited, it simply states that you're going for it. It eliminates pressure and judgment and lets you, well, Go for it!

Anxiety About Anxiety Causes Anxiety

There was an eight-year-old crying at after-school pick up. She was almost hysterical, racing back and forth, saying she wanted to go home, and that she was afraid. I asked the counselor what was going on and it seemed the young girl had an untied shoe lace and felt she was going to die as a result. The counselor kept telling her to stop crying, that she wasn't going to die, there was nothing to be afraid of and to stop it. This just increased the child's hysteria.

I walked over and said, "It's ok to be afraid. It can be scary." Immediately, she stopped crying and looked at me. I said. "Can you breathe in through your nose and out through your mouth like me?" and I began to breathe slowly, modeling what I wanted her to do. She began to do it, eyes locked with mine. We breathed together and mellowed the beast of anxiety.

I write this not as a kudos to me, but as a show of compassion for people who experience any level of anxiety. It is a nasty companion.

I believe that the young girl truly felt that she was going to die and here's why: her heart was probably pounding incredibly fast; her head was probably hurting from clenching her jaw; she was jumpy and probably felt out of control. All of these symptoms of anxiety can be terrifying, which just increases the anxiety.

Anxiety about anxiety causes anxiety.

The fastest way to manage anxiety is to breathe. Slowly and steadily. And walk through your body: is my heart racing? Check. Is my head hurting? Check. Am I sweating? Check. Thank you, body, for showing me I need to get more oxygen to my brain. Breathe.

Oxygen to the brain slows down the train of anxiety, and allows us to see things a bit more clearly.

That high-pitched hysteria you were feeling is now ebbing to a softer edginess. The more you breathe, the gentler you feel. You're in charge now; anxiety is no longer driving the bus.

And talk to yourself the way I spoke to that young girl. No judgment. "It's ok to be scared." I didn't agree or disagree that there was something to be afraid of; I allowed her to feel what she was feeling. I didn't fight her anxiety; I invited it to the table. And in that gesture, anxiety released its grip.

Give yourself the gifts of breathing and no judgment. Share this with your family, friends, coworkers- anyone you know who has slight or more intense anxiety. I don't propose that medication is unnecessary. In fact medication can be amazing. But relying on medication alone can feed the feeling of helplessness so many anxiety sufferers experience. It's empowering, and immediately effective, to be an active participant in managing anxiety.

You've got the power.

You Should Not Read This

Nothing will suck your spirit dry more than a "should." Shoulds are the evil voice of a critic telling you what you must do in order to be loved. They're a constant statement of "You're not enough as you are." They can come from well-intentioned colleagues, neighbors, friends, or your very own Inner Critic. (There she is again!)

People try to "help" by suggesting ways to Be. How to dress, where to live, what job to take…feel free to add your own. This "help" is well intentioned and that's nice sometimes. But whether it's welcome advice or not, it's what we do with this information that separates the unhappy child from the happy adult. I used to buckle under the pressure of the Shoulds whether they came from outside or inside my head. I'd either do the thing grudgingly or avoid doing it and feel guilty. Neither choice fed my spirit. I was so busy trying to please others, including my inner critic, to win their affection by doing what they recommended, that I didn't know who I was or what I wanted. Well, that's not entirely true. I knew deep down what I wanted, but I was afraid of trusting my instinct. What if I did what I wanted and failed? Then they'd be justified in saying "I told you so." It took me many years to realize that if I did fail, it was with passion and purpose and in alignment with my own definition of greatness.

The change happened when I started to replace the "sh" in "should" with a "c" for "could." It was magical! It changed a directive into a choice. It wasn't that I should do it, it was that I could choose to do it. Below are some before and after thought patterns straight from my life. Notice I start with "I" because even if 10 people suggested I should do something, it's up to me to own this chatter in my head.

From "I should read that book!" to "I could read during my commute."

From "I should exercise!" to "I could do yoga at home."

From "I should take better care of myself!" to "I could try kale."

Now doesn't "could" feel better? It opens doors of opportunity to what we want to do rather than what we think we have to do. That simple change from "sh" to "c" reduces stress quickly and effectively, and it's available 24/7.

The language we choose is a door to freedom. It's a path to our deepest knowing and most joyous life. It's up to us to choose our words wisely and honor our heart in our day to day.

May you find the path that nurtures You.

Perfectionism Paralysis

Perfectionism is simply fear. It can be fear of failure or fear of success, or fear of vulnerability or fear of fame. Regardless, the result is inertia. Does this feel familiar?

I call it Perfection Paralysis (P2 for short) and it's one of my greatest challenges. There's a red flag that goes up in my belly when I slide into P2. I might moan about my P2, or justify why I'm not good enough to do what I committed to do, or resign myself to my debilitating P2 and watch TED videos while feeling guilty. But whining and guilt are a distraction from doing the real work of facing our fears head on and then delivering a Good Enough product.

To a Perfectionist, "good enough" feels like they're delivering at 80%, yet it's most people's 110%. This means that most, if not all, of our bosses are wowed by 80% from us. I'm not suggesting we lower our standards and deliver work we're not proud of; I am suggesting we cut ourselves some slack and eliminate P2.

Consider this fact: Your intention versus what is perceived is beyond our control. Know your audience. You may put in 100% of your perfectionist energy into a presentation and have your boss slice and dice it because she consistently needs to have her thumbprint on anything that leaves her department. That's not good management but it's everywhere. So what do we perfectionists do? Pick and choose where to put 80% effort and where to invest more.

I can hear some you saying, "But people will know when I'm not putting in 100%!" It's ok if people recognize that you aren't delivering your all at all times. That's an unrealistic expectation. Human beings require downtime to recharge. Look around and start noticing who is giving what, and when. I'm guessing that pretty quickly you'll see how energy ebbs and flows throughout a team of people. That's a lot of what collaboration is about; helping each other recharge and keep momentum going simultaneously. We can let perfectionism freeze us or we can create our best "good enough" and move forward.

And a word about perfectionism and this book: There is no benefit to setting an expectation of 100% mastery of what's written in this book. This is a guideline and each of us must find our own way to the inner knowing required to be the leader we're all capable of being.

The Comparer's Prison

Typos are an interesting phenomenon, especially the ones we make over and over. I make the same typo every time I type the word comparison; I end up typing comaprison. At first I was annoyed, then intrigued, and finally I realized they are the very same thing.

When I hear that chatter of "not good enough" going on in my head, it's a sure bet I'm comparing myself to someone. How else can I be "not enough" unless I'm comparing myself to the other "better" person? When I get caught up in the story it's telling me, I'm in a kind of prison. A coma of wishing I were not me.

Have you ever felt this way? Of course you haven't, you're perfect. In my mind, you have it all and are happy in every area of your life, at all times. My coma-prison mind tells me that if only I were as good as you, I'd be happy also. This coma-prison minds affects us at work, home, on the playground, and on vacation. That's the dance we comparers do to ourselves. First we compare ourselves to someone. Then we make up a story about them and their perfect life. Then we say, "See? I knew it. I'm not good enough."

The inner critic, or IC as I like to refer to my special friend, is what leads us down the comparison path. She is so creative! She finds endless ways to compare me to people who, were I in charge, I wouldn't care about. But since my IC is running the show, all of a sudden I care deeply about the fact that they're better at math, or excel, or sucking up. Seriously, do I really care if someone else is better at sucking up? Apparently I do, at this moment. But only because I'm letting my IC lead me to the coma prison of comparison. My normally active and passionate brain settles into a drugged state of compliance. I'm a coma prison zombie doing the not-good-enough zombie dance.

Does the dance feed something? Is it easier to just beat ourselves up? I'm going with yes on this one because we all do it. It's hard to fight the mind; it doesn't work to tell our IC to shut up. So we interpret the endless chatter as the truth when it really isn't. I want to repeat that.

The endless chatter is not the truth. It is our Inner Critic demanding attention; that is all.

If we could just quiet the mind, we'd be golden. But that's so incredibly outrageously unrealistic. No one can do that; not even the Dalai Lama. So what's our option? Yet again, we invite the inner critic to the table. "You want my attention? Fine then, come sit down. Let's chat."

I am, in fact, suggesting that you talk with yourself. Consider doing this in a private location so as not to disturb others. But do have a chat with your IC.

Break down the accusations of lesser than, dissect the threats of pending doom she holds over your head, and contextualize these observations of betterness. Once you do this, you will organically diffuse the anger she makes you feel. When the anger evaporates, the truth shows up all shiny and bright. You don't envy his ability to suck up, her ability to please the boss or that person's prowess with Excel. (Ok, maybe Excel. It would be awesome to master Excel.) It's like clouds parting from your drugged brain and suddenly you can see clearly now. Peace descends and you see your true value in the world, and at work.

The more aware we are of the coma prison effect, the faster we get at recognizing our IC at work, and the faster we get at cutting through her drama and zooming straight to our truth. What's your truth?

setting boundaries

People will take advantage of us until we set boundaries. Each time we jump like a bunny to respond, we're reinforcing their view of us as a scared rabbit. When we're consistently willing to work late, always be available, come in when sick, or do their work for them. Or when we allow someone to repeatedly berate us publicly. Or when we accept the limits placed on us by others. It's up to us to diplomatically and intelligently set boundaries, for ourselves and for others.

Compassion Does Not Equal Doormat

Beverly's boss reprimanded her in public rather than have constructive conversations in private. He would try to bait her with personal questions and then make fun when she faltered. And sometimes he'd even take her ideas and present them as his own.

Have you been there? Are you there now? I have and I can tell you it's no fun. It's time to set boundaries, diplomatically and tenaciously. Often, people think compassion means being easily manipulated. It does NOT mean that. Having compassion for our self and for others means being aware of what we, and they, are going through. It does not mean letting people run over us. Therefore, setting boundaries with compassion means defining a line that cannot be crossed without consequences. The consequences may be profound or minor, but as long as there are clear and diplomatic consequences, people will respect the line. They may not like it, but they'll have to respect it or pay the consequences. (In some cases, they may appreciate the clearly delineated border. Most people thrive in a structured environment and find relief in knowing where the boundaries are. Even not-so-nice people.)

Here's how to set boundaries:

1. Don't focus on changing him. You can yell at him or hug him; he is where he is on his journey. We can't assume we know

what someone else needs to do to be happy (and therefore nice) and, frankly, it's distracting us from taking care of ourselves.

2. DO focus on You. What do you need?

   a. Advocates. Reach out to your senior manager and your HR partner and calmly state what you're experiencing. No defensive whining. Just the facts, ma'am. Consider putting these facts into the bucket of how inefficient it is for the company rather than how infuriating it is to you personally.

   b. Clarity. Put it in writing. You may never share these notes with anyone, but it clarifies our experience and fortifies our ability to speak with calm authority about the history of a challenging relationship.

   c. Authority. Holding your head high and shoulders back, schedule a meeting with the offending person and calmly call him on his behavior. If he denies it, state that if he persists, there will be action taken.

3. Compassion. For him and for you.

   a. Have compassion for his struggle. When we consider what may be driving his childish behavior, we realize that it has nothing to do with us. We're just the recipients of his own feeling of lack. This makes it not personal, which is much easier to manage.

   b. Say it out loud to yourself or your non-work confidante. "This is pissing me off! I just want to do good work and this person is distracting me and dragging my name through the mud." Wow, that feels good. It's validating to state out loud what we're experiencing because it's undeniably infuriating. And that validation is a release of toxic energy enabling the clean energy to flow and energize us.

We're always in the position of leadership, formally or not. It's up to us to model that compassion does not mean being a doormat. Our responsibility is to ourselves, and to those who see how we lead our teams and our careers.

Compassion does not mean being a doormat.

Quiet Confidence Wins

Chances are you've had a manager who sits on the far left or right on the Confidence Scale. I'll explain.

On the far left is the Mousey Cautious Meek Tentative Timid Uncertain manager. She's exhausting because she's so busy trying to get you to like her that she never truly leads. Her passivity leaves you wondering what your priorities are and you end up deciding for yourself, hoping you're doing the right thing. She doesn't advocate for you because she doesn't know how to advocate for herself much less anyone else. She is driven by fear that someone will find out she's got nothing to offer.

On the far right is the Cocky Arrogant Presumptuous Conceited Egotistical manager. She's a pain in the rear because she steals your ideas and presents them as her own. She yells and talks down at you and your peers. You just can't win. She uses smoke and mirrors to cover for the fact that she doesn't actually contribute much to the party. Like her counterpart on the left, she is driven by fear that someone will find out she's got nothing to offer.

We've all worked for one or both of these characters and chances are high that we've been one of them at some point in our careers. It's natural to feel like an impostor when you start managing and it can be terrifying. It gets confusing – do I make a show of bravado or do I sit in the back row and wait to be called on? And it can be exhausting to be a seasoned manager who's been treated poorly for years. What models are out there for me if all I've experienced is nastiness? And so the question is, what kind of manager do I want to be? Since you're reading this book, I'm guessing you want to be neither the mouse nor the jerk. And so I introduce the Quiet Confidence of a compassionate manager.

A Compassionate Manager leads with the whole truth, is neither mousy nor cocky, but quietly confident.

Quiet confidence means pausing before we react to think it through. To connect with ourselves, and with the reason we're reacting. This requires compassion and honesty:

"Do I want to scream because I'm embarrassed I didn't know?"
"Am I whispering because I don't believe I'm ready to be a manager?"
"Am I ready to yell because the accusation may damage my

reputation?"

Quiet confidence is acceptance of: not knowing, feeling afraid, or being defensive. It's the recognition that no one is perfect, no matter how old or young they are. We all have to learn and make mistakes and that it's the openness about our mistakes that makes us a Compassionate Manager.

This humility makes space for our direct reports and colleagues, and even our superiors, to also fall on their faces, then get up and go for it again, having learned from their mistake. It's laughing at ourselves AND taking it seriously when we mess up.

This is a boundary we are setting. It's as if we're saying, "I recognize what my error and I'm going to make sure it doesn't happen again." And when we teach our team to hold themselves accountable with quiet confidence, we are setting boundaries of how and when we need to redirect their behavior. Managers do not want to babysit, and managees don't want to be babysat. It's a win-win for everyone.

Turn a Personal Attack into a Statement of Fact

You're not in charge of facilities, but your boss screams at you about the lack of toilet paper in the bathroom. You reply:

1. "I'm not in charge of that! Don't yell at me!"
2. "I didn't know. I'm sorry, I didn't realize. I'll go buy some right now."

3. "Would you like me to call facilities?"

Answer 1 is in the heat of the moment. The screaming match is now about how you treat each other. It has nothing to do with toilet paper or job responsibilities at all.

Answer 2 is when we're feeling unsure of our job stability. We assume responsibility for an absurd thing (toilet paper!) because we're terrified of showing our boss that he's off his rocker.

Answer 3 is Turning A Personal Attack Into A Statement Of Fact. In this scenario, it's respectfully not taking ownership of an absurd thing.

Turning A Personal Attack Into A Statement Of Fact is the art of diplomatically not taking the bait.

Toilet paper is an easy scenario to not take personally (unless of course you are in facilities). It gets hard to stay unemotional when the attack is about something that could be a mistake on your part.

The best way to manage our emotional response is to start identifying the trigger that sets us all off: tone of voice. The slightly high-pitched, whiny tone with an edge. Yes, that one. I'm guilty of it; we all are at some point. We're triggering others when we do it and others trigger us. Develop your flag for this tone and you'll be able to choose between emotional response or a respectful statement of fact.

Compassionate Management

"Why is this project late?!"

Emotional: "Susan didn't get the data on time! It wasn't me!"

Statement of Fact: "I've just received the data and the deliverables will be ready by 9am tomorrow."

When is the report going to be ready?!

Emotional: "Thursday! I told you it would be ready on Thursday and it will!"

Statement of Fact: "On Thursday as promised."

How did you come to that conclusion?!

Emotional: "I, um, I, well I…"

Statement of Fact: "It makes sense to me and here's why:…"

Often times, people who bait others will wince when we don't bite. They may even up the ante. It's exhausting! Our job is to stay neutral and continue answering factually. We may even name what's going on if it gets too intense by saying, "I'm not biting the hook you're dangling. I've answered each of your questions and am getting back to work now." Remember the chapter we're in right now is called Setting Boundaries. Staying factual is a boundary-setting action.

It's how we separate the emotion from the fact that gives us the ability to stay focused on the topic and not get caught up in the spiral of emotion. Now you are in charge of setting the tone of the communication style, and as a result, the relationship.

Talk about Power.

Communication Style Matters

Do you ever feel like you present great ideas and they get shot down, ignored, eye-rolled, or squashed? And then you feel demotivated to keep trying to be creative, thoughtful, and forward-thinking? Let's assume you have smart, thoughtful, on-brand ideas that align with the company strategy. Why do they keep being shot down? It's easy to go straight to "why does my boss always shoot ME down?" That's Taking It Personally. Instead of making it personal, consider that it's most likely the boss's thang. If we're going to stay in the job, it's up to us to figure it out.

In the Not Taking It Personally formula, step 3 is so important that we're going to focus on it now:

Step #1. Recognize when we're taking it personally

Step #2. Define the meaning we are applying

Step #3. Factualize it

Step #4. Move forward

Getting to the facts is a discovery process that takes time and insight. Be honest with yourself. Even jerks don't want to keep dissing ideas. They always want to be right and smarter and the ruler, but they don't want to keep saying no. So if you're noticing an increase in frustration on the part of your boss, you are most likely repeating a core "wrong" theme throughout your ideas. Somehow it's triggering your boss and now she's in an anticipatory and therefore self-fulfilling cycle. She's going to find fault no matter what you present because the core "wrong" thing hasn't been addressed.

In looking at why someone reacts to us in a certain way, we must look at what and how we are presenting the information.

Is the content we present appropriate? Read these examples and see if any resonate. Content is half the puzzle.

Are you a visionary and your boss isn't? That equals perceived off-target ideas and can be experienced as you trying to make her look bad.

Do you repeatedly suggest solutions that are out of budget because you believe in them? Doing this every now and again shows passion; overdoing it dilutes your credibility and can be perceived as not caring about the bottom line.

Do you state your idea as if it was just so obvious and everyone in the room is an idiot? We've all done this.

Do you ask the same questions repeatedly, just to be absolutely sure? That conveys fear, insecurity, and lack of intelligence, not the detailed and thorough perception you were hoping for. Some things can be assumed (yes I said assumed!) on projects that happen repeatedly.

Maybe it's not the ideas itself but how they're being presented. How we present information is the other half. Note when an idea is embraced and when it isn't. Dissect your boss's reaction.

Words, body language, tone of voice – it's all data for your investigation. At what point did the sigh of exasperation occur? At what sentence did the refusal to hear you out begin? Does she communicate bullet-point style or with meandering details? Watch how she responds to others, and learn from their interactions. And then try different approaches. Maybe even ask her what style she prefers. Here are some approaches that work quite well:

Present ideas in such a way that the boss thinks it was her idea. This is a universal managing-up approach that is both exasperating and truly effective.

Be selective about what time of day to present ideas. If you must present in the afternoon, bring almonds and chocolate (healthy energy boost and pure sugar work well).

Look for trigger words. Many people have them. If you pay close attention, you can identify these words and avoid them. Does she take a deep breath each time you mention dogs? Wince when you say balloons? Shudder when you say ice cream? Trigger words can be anything at all, so watch for body reactions.

Be attentive to what's on her schedule. Interrupting someone never goes well; especially the catching her in the hallway fyi. She'll only focus on not being late for her next meeting.

It's important to recognize where our actions and reactions are contributing to our being shut down, because then we can shift our behavior to redirect our boss's reaction.

When we identify the source of angst, we can be in control of the communication style and avoid the angst entirely.

The Mistreater's Journey

Here's the thing about mistreatment:

It's real.

It's unnecessary.

And it has little to do with those who are being mistreated.

The Mistreater's furiously bubbling stew of fears and insecurities are overflowing onto the mistreated. It's the Mistreater's Journey and you happen to be in its path at that moment.

When the boss yells at the employee, chances are astronomically high that the boss is struggling with a fear of being seen as less than powerful, or his job may be on the line, or he may be constipated. We may never know the real reason for the explosion. The same is true in family or romantic dynamics. We may never understand why he spoke to you that way or why your brother is cold or why she broke up with no warning. Or we may one day find out. We just don't know right now. What we do know is that the Mistreater is going through something not-so-fun. She may appear to be friendly, fun, full of laughter to others, but look into her eyes and see if you can find the truth. There's likely a deep sadness.

We may trigger the mistreatment unknowingly, but that doesn't make us responsible for it.

Our job is not to help the Mistreater; our job is to set boundaries to protect ourselves. Compassion is the way to do it. Find compassion for him even if he treats us like poop. Why? Because this will help us get through the day. We also need to find endless compassion for ourselves for being on the receiving end of said poop.

The Mistreater's Journey is a lonely one and it can only be fixed by the Mistreater. Have you been here? Do you remember wondering how you could have said that thing; acted that way; walked out at that moment? We've all mistreated and hopefully we've all felt bad about it and apologized. What's important when you are the Mistreated is to find that shared experience and tap into the feeling you had in your tummy when you did it. This will be your bridge to compassion for the colleague who throws you under the bus.

When we find compassion for our offender, we are tapping into our endless capacity for love. It makes the heart fill like the Grinch's, and the anger recedes a bit. It's a healing poultice for ourselves.

Are you thinking- does she really want me to find compassion for that jerk who spread rumors about me at work? Yes, I do. Get quiet, look inward to that time you yelled at direct report. Feel the shame, then feel the hurt that led you to do it. Now find compassion for the You at that moment. Let's give the offender the Benefit of the Doubt and guess that she's feeling the same series of emotions – from shame to sadness to regret. Let's offer her compassion.

And even when we find compassion for our mistreater, the anger doesn't go away, nor should it. Anger is a healthy emotion and beautifully powerful when used correctly. It's professionally calling out the bus thrower. Taking action while acknowledging anger and compassion for the offender, and for your beautiful Self, will lead to calm and therefore a happier you. Ultimately you may need to find a new job, but take your time and see if this boundary setting tool helps you shift what seemed untenable into a manageable situation..

The final word on this is that we can't fix mistreaters. We have a responsibility to protect ourselves and still thrive at our work. We set the boundaries of letting the offenders actions get to us by using compassion as a buffer. Throw in a little Not Taking It personally and we've got a strong boundary keeping us safe and solid.

Compassion Is NOT The Most Important Tool

It's true. Compassion is an incredible tool, a way of thinking, a way of being. But it takes energy for those of us who are still practicing and learning. So you can't deliver compassion without energy. And food only goes so far.

It's sleep. Yes, I said it. I, the biggest breaker of this rule. But

I have so much to do! I have a long list! I have blah blah blah.

Here's my own experience; tell me if this resonates with you.

When I get 8+ hours of sleep, things roll off my back easier. I don't take things personally. I can see other people's perspectives before they even need to explain.

When I get 6 hours of sleep, I need to remind myself not to take things personally. I lose my cool and rein it in quickly. I have to work at seeing other points of view.

When I get 5 hours of sleep, I'm angry. Grumpy. Curt. Impatient. I think everyone is an idiot.

And when I get 5-6 hours of sleep a few nights in a row, steer clear, please. Mama's not a happy camper.

What does sleep have to do with setting boundaries? Everything. When we set a boundary for taking care of our bodies, we are also taking care of our minds. Well-rested minds deliver great work.

There are few things we can control in this universe. One thing we can control is when to lie down. And then we can also decide to do a guided meditation or deep, slow breathing exercise or count sheep.

Don't underestimate rest. It's a beautiful gift we can give ourselves. Rest the body, rest the mind, rest the heart. Rest is a gentle segue to sleep and, for most of us, we need to rest before we can drift off to sleep.

When we make time for resting our body and mind, we are better leaders.

I know I'm a better leader/colleague/manager when I get enough sleep. So why don't I take this seriously? I'm too tired to answer that.

Here's my theory. Like the patient who starts to feel better and stops taking the last of the antibiotic only to have the infection return, we get lazy about taking care of ourselves. What's a few hours here and there? And then it builds up and we get cranky and make mistakes and suddenly we're in bed by 8pm to catch up. Roller-coaster sleep – from deprivation to indulgence.

Maybe we also feel guilty about sleeping when there's so much to be done. But like the oxygen mask on an airplane, we must take care of ourselves in order to most effectively and efficiently take care of others. Compassionate Managers care about their team and colleagues. We empower them to bring their best efforts to work, so we must model self care daily.

Boasting about working all night on a project is the way a manager tells the team she expects her team to do the same. It's also telling the team to expect the manager to fix their mistakes at night. It's un-empowering and invasive. People want work-life balance. That requires setting boundaries and getting sleep.

If we want to be our best in all interactions, we need sleep. It's scientifically proven and easy to test. Sufficient sleep is a simple boundary to set for ourselves, our colleagues, and our families.

Post-Traumatic Job Disorder

The name will make you giggle and giggling is good. But the affliction is real and many suffer from it.

Fear-based management is prevalent. Think about your work environments over the years. How many times have you felt beaten down, thrown your hands in the air with futility, exhausted? It's not healthy, for the person, the department or the business.

Working in an environment where individuality and creativity are shut down leads to Post-Traumatic Job Disorder, or PTJD.

Why is this in a book about Compassionate Management? Because a department leader must be able to recognize signs of trauma in order to advocate for those in need. The intention is to ensure it doesn't happen, and that requires proactive action. Clarifying what is and what is not acceptable. Does your company have an Ethical Standards Agreement? Find out, use it, and make one for your team that aligns with it. Be like an eagle on the hunt to ensure that these standards are not crossed. Make it safe for people to call out questions and share confidential concerns.

And in those instances where we're human and we miss something until the damage has been done? Take immediate and unwavering action. For example, bullying is prevalent. People can't be discriminatory anymore which is great, but that has led to a passive-aggressive game that goes on and it's dangerous. It may even take a while to identify certain behaviors as some form of bullying. But once it is identified, it's the leaders job to enforce boundaries. This applies to all forms of trauma, bullying just being an easy example.

The associate needs to set boundaries; the manager must be a true advocate in enforcing these boundaries.

Once we experience something, we can't un-experience it. A work trauma can take many forms:

- The CEO yells and paces with rage at you for reasons you don't understand
- Every time you present an idea, you get shut down
- Someone throws you under the bus and no one advocates for you
- The department head consistently tries to humiliate you publicly
- You work for Jekyl and Hyde, so you never know what to expect
- What would you add here? The list is personal and lengthy.

PTJD leads back to one source: Trust betrayed. Even though we don't say to our new boss, "Hey, I'm trusting you to be respectful towards me," we still feel betrayed when she isn't.

We walk in innocent. We anticipate our boss and colleagues

will want to collaborate, partner, and help each other. I have never met someone who walks into a job looking forward to being treated like poop. It doesn't matter how many years we work; we almost always enter a new work relationship with hope. We hope for a trusting, open environment where we will feel valued, seen and understood.

Let me be clear here: hope is a gift. It's a miracle of humankind to be ever hopeful. It would be horrible if we gave up hope. I shudder to think what life would be like if we stopped dating, trying new foods, reading new books. The same applies to work. We keep trying to find a company where our Self is appreciated, where we can contribute our highest level of contribution to the greater good.

So what to do when we are, or someone on our team is, smacked down? This is where boundary-setting is so useful. Boundaries set from the beginning give us a marker of how far someone has crossed the line. It enables us to hold the offender accountable and reach out to our Human Resources partner to get support with a clearly delineated unacceptable situation. We change the situation and hold the offender accountable to cease the offensive actions.

There's another boundary to address. What if we can't change the situation? Do we stay or move on? These are deeply personal questions we must address in private. The bottom line is that we must do everything we can to avoid PTJD, and to protect our teams from it. It's much harder to undo trauma if you've been traumatized repeatedly over a period of time.

The sooner we remove ourselves from the traumatic situation, the quicker we will begin to heal.

Trauma can strip away a sense of our own talents and gifts; our strengths become distorted into perceived weaknesses. I've seen so many talented and skilled people consider themselves unhire-able because of what a previous (or current) boss was saying to them.

People who inflict trauma on others can sense innocence and hope. They're like tigers prowling prey. It's up to us to develop our radar and prevent these attacks from reaching our team or our own soul. We can't always prevent the attacks, but we can prevent them from affecting us deeply by taking action that has been enabled by setting boundaries.

thriving during difficult times

Difficult times can bring out the best or the worst in us. It takes a conscious effort to deliver our best and not sink into the common response of fear. It's natural to feel a lack of control when the going is rough. I'm guilty of sinking back into fear, we all are. Let's be real about this. Compassionate Management can be a breeze when everyone is aligned and feels safe. It's when the road gets bumpy that Fear-Based Management rears its ugly head. When people are scared, they fight or flight. Compassion helps us connect to what we're feeling, and what the team may be feeling, so we can speak to it with authority. Fear is not driving the bus; clarity is. It's our responsibility to help others through transition with compassion, and to help ourselves as well.

Embracing What Is

Sometimes we get on a plane to Paris and end up in Holland. You signed up for crepes and red wine. Instead you're looking at tulips. Miles and miles of tulips.*

Do you know what I'm talking about? You thought you were going to be a ballet dancer with the New York City ballet but instead you're a fashion designer with a hot brand. It's not that you didn't want to be a designer, it's that you still lament the loss of the ballet life. Or maybe you wanted to be a TV personality and you're the VP of Training and Development at an international firm. Or you wanted to be a novelist and you're an advertising copywriter.

Our talents can take us many places, and sometimes life forces a direction on us. That's when we end up in tulip land. Holland can be permanent for some – like the broken bone for the ballet dancer, or TBD – like the great opportunity for the HR star, or temporary – like the need for steady income for the copywriter.

It's how we choose to experience What Is that makes it a fun or dismal experience. It's our choice.

The Permanent scenario is hard on the ballet dancer, but the finality of it can be freeing. He will never be young again and he will always have the remains of the injury, but he will always have creativity, vision, and grace. These same talents have made him quite the success in the fashion industry.

The TBD scenario is quite fun. Do I or don't I want to go back to what I was pursuing or am I having so much fun in this new and unexpected world? It's a giddy feeling to have the freedom to soar at something new and not have to decide your next move. (I wish this for everyone!)

The Temporary scenario: It's hard to put dreams on hold. On the other hand, food and shelter are good. The hardest part here is the unknown. We don't know when or how we'll be able to get back to our dream and that not-knowing can churn our insides. So we've got to make a radical choice. Do I stay with my sadness and feelings of failure or do I say, "Screw that! I choose to embrace where I am, on a path I never expected. I'm both apprehensive and excited about where it'll take me."

Based on personal experience, I recommend embracing What Is with all your heart. The more we fight it, the more we stay stagnant. We get more and more stuck in the mud and it gets harder and harder to get out. The downward cycle feeds off itself. But so does the upward cycle. Energy flows when we embrace where we are and this allows for incredible and wondrous experiences we didn't expect.

How willing are you to accept your version of Holland or help your team accept and embrace their Holland? This is our responsibility to ourselves and to our colleagues. If you're feeling sad, embarrassed, or even ashamed about ending up in Holland instead of Paris, use that emotion as a motivation to find compassion for yourself. It can be really hard. I understand this deeply. Now that you've recognized your sadness, it's time to take action. How can you make this ok-ish or even great? It is magical when we own our power and change how we react to something unexpected.

Compassionate Managers know the value of embracing What Is, taking steps to improve it as best as we can, and moving forward from there.

Welcome to Holland. The tulips are magical.

* This is my interpretation of the "Welcome to Holland" essay by Emily Perl Kingsley.

Changing Our Thinking

Change is bleeping hard. Change is challenging because it requires changing our thinking. That's the hardest part. Compassion is the tool to use to change our thinking. When we cut ourselves some slack, it creates breathing room for What Is and enables us to see clearly what our next steps can be. It's hard, and do-able. We're not changing who we are or what we want; we're simply changing how we think about the situation.

Imagine you went for a promotion. You knew you were more qualified than your colleague who was also going for it. But he plays sneaky and manipulative and he got it. Ouch, that burns. Now what? Do you wallow in bitter, resentful, and angry? I get that, but it eats up your energy and sends out icky vibes.

How do we change our thinking?

Compare yourself to You. I do not recommend comparing yourself to others, but we all do it at times. Some people beat themselves up by comparing to someone "more" successful than them. Others use it as away to feel better about their situation by comparing to those less fortunate. Either approach is superficial. Superficial stays on the top level of our epidermis, it doesn't sink into the heart, which means the comfort won't last either. But when you compare yourself to yourself, you're doing the correct measurement. Am I where I want to be? Now you can define where you want to be. Powerful.

Fight no more. Oh boy, I fight change like a pro and I'm exhausted to prove it. Have you ever felt so angry and pissed off at the universe or whomever is running this darn show called life? That's called fighting it. I'm not saying you shouldn't be angry, not at all. I'm saying that if you are frozen and unable to take action, you're fighting what needs to happen. Release and all will flow. If not beautifully, then definitely less painfully.

Talk it up. The tool to avoid the truth of what's really going on is to not discuss it with anyone. There's no need to announce it to the world, but there is a huge benefit to bouncing off ideas with someone you trust and who has your best interest at heart. It's amazing what happens when we speak words aloud. Suddenly we can see things in a different perspective and that's where the change starts.

Name the coexisting truths. It's both infuriating that he got the promotion AND if that's what's being rewarded, maybe you dodged a bullet by not being chosen for that role.

Take responsibility for your own happiness. It starts inside. For real. Regardless of what is being flung at you, own your power, your courage, and your potential for greatness.

Gratitude. This is the most powerful tool in the universe. Compassion leads to gratitude, which is the ultimate gift to yourself. Say "Thank you" as often as you want and you'll start to feel thankful. List the things you are thankful for – your toes that wiggle, your brain that can think, your friends, the list is truly endless.

Take action. Yes! Positive, self-fulfilling, forward momentum action. Update your resume. Research companies to find the right fit. Or take inside-your-company action. I know someone who didn't "get the promotion" and she used her energy to take a leadership role in the Women's Initiative at her company. She has since had exposure to world leaders and received an award of recognition for her service.

Our world cannot change without a change in our thinking.

How we experience something is 100% based on our perception. The facts of a situation are simply facts. They only carry the meaning we give them.

Do you have friends who see the glass half empty, or full? It's the same glass of water. It's their perception that changes how they experience it. The same applies to change at work such as disappointment about a project or promotion or… Changing our perception changes how we experience it. We have the power to do this repeatedly, and this tool never runs out of fuel. There will be countless opportunities to hone this skill, and it's magnificent when we master it. It's freeing and energizing to start out angry and end up empowered.

When To Share Gossip

Why am I writing about gossip in the Thriving During Difficult Times section? Because difficult times are scary, and when we're scared, we gossip. It's a way of trying to control what's beyond out control. Rumors become the main source of information as people begin to panic. Rough periods are a gossip swamp, and it happens when we managers don't disseminate information appropriately.

The first time I was trusted with information about someone's poor performance review, I came really close to warning her. I remember the relief when I heard that they had changed their minds and she was fine. I also remember the flood of "Holy Sh*t! I almost told her!" That would have been disastrous for everyone. Over the years, I was told that so-and-so would be fired, that guy would be promoted and you-know-who would be demoted. I was told that she'd get a raise. I was told that the company was going to sink like the titanic. And I was told that he was sleeping with her and would be transferred as a result. None of these very real scenarios turned out as expected. There was always a last-minute change of mind by someone. Alternatively, there have been many cases where the confidential information shared with me did come to pass. But I never knew which would and which wouldn't.

Rumors are untrustworthy and spreading them makes you untrustworthy.

If you feel guilty about knowing your boss's intention to completely overhaul the department, keep in mind we never really know how it will play out. It's amazing how things shift and move when change is afoot. It's unpredictable and scary at times, and it's not your responsibility to communicate for your boss.

On the other hand, if someone comes to you and asks about the validity of the gossip they've heard, it's ok to acknowledge that you've heard it also and that you don't know if it will come to fruition. It can be crazy-making when a boss pretends something is unreal; it makes it even scarier for the associate.

There was a rumor that we were being bought by a bigger company and that layoffs were imminent. When my direct report asked me if this was true, I said I didn't know. I told him that although it was possible, I had lived through this before and guessed that the company would keep our department as they had no expertise in what we did. It was an honest and hopeful answer and gave my direct report comfort.

When someone confides in us, treat it as confidential. If they then want to tell everyone, that's their party. And if someone accuses you of withholding information, show them compassion and educate them; explain how unpredictable rumors really are. They're scared and don't know whom to trust. Show them that you are trustworthy by being trustworthy.

H.B.O.S.

Years ago I was working in a toxic company. The culture was one of backstabbing and sneakiness and misery.

So I left and everything was roses and unicorns! Kidding.

I stayed at that job because I needed the income. There are a lot of us who've had to do this and might have to do it again. There are a few tricks we can employ to help make an unpleasant situation palatable. I don't mean fun; I mean manageable, acceptable or satisfactory enough to stay for a while.

Trick #1

Create a ball that's labeled H.B.O.S. (that's Hot Bag of Sh*t). You see, I was given many bags of hot excrement at the toxic job and I was expected to hand them off to my team with a smile. It was unpleasant to say the least. So I came up with the idea for a ball labeled H.B.O.S..

Trick #2

Laugh. We laugh when we see someone else laughing and that makes us feel GOOD! Google "laugh" and watch all the babies and puppies and kittens you need. Buy a joke book and read it to yourself. Rent silly movies at night and think of the hilarious scenes during a boring meeting. Laughter is the best medicine for a broken spirit.

Trick #3

Find a colleague whom you can trust and do NOT bitch about work. Ok, a little whining is fine. But if complaining is all you do, that's all the friendship is about and that's not a friendship. In other words, the bitching relationship will take you in a downward spiral of unhappiness and make you dislike everyone around you, maybe because you'll sense them avoiding your company. Instead, reach out with joy and develop friendships that will nurture your soul and feed you energy and elevate you above the crumminess around you.

H.B.O.S. stands for "Hot Bag of Sh*t," but it can explained as "How to Blow Off Steam." Anytime I was handed a steaming HBOS, I called my one trusted colleague and we tossed the ball around for a bit. Until we laughed.

It can be crushingly disappointing to have to stay somewhere miserable, but we have the power to change our inner experience and make it through. At least until we find the job with roses and unicorns.

Buh-Bye Blame Game

When things go wrong at the office, it's easy to point a finger. So easy in fact that it's the default action. It's also counterproductive. Finger-pointing creates an atmosphere of fear that destroys trust. It's helpful to identify what went wrong, but I propose that instead of playing the blame game, we adopt a different attitude:

It's no one person's fault and it's everyone's responsibility.

Generally speaking, a flop of some sort requires multiple failed factors along the way. Whether you're creating a shoe, a brochure, or a hedge fund, your product goes through a lifecycle of creation. Step by step, the product starts as a concept and then ultimately becomes a tangible finished item for customer consumption. This is called the Concept-to-Completion Lifecycle. In this lifecycle, there are multiple touch points with different people contributing their piece of the whole.

Let's step back a bit and look at these people contributing their piece of the whole. In the abstract conversation of employee expectation, it's easy to say we expect a commitment to deliver 100% at all times. But we know our game cannot possibly be at one consistent level at all times, and certainly not at the highest level of all. A smart manager knows that the best scenario is when team members even each other out. (A is having a low-energy day; B is having a high-energy day.)

What this means is that if there are 10 touch points in the lifecycle of that product, it's possible that 5 of them are low-energy and 5 are high. We're all counting on the high-energy folks to catch things missed by low-energy.

This is true teamwork: people helping each other without question. There is no back-stabbing here; they have each other's backs. They look out for one another and for the product.

They live the motto: It's no one person's fault and it's everyone's responsibility.

helping ourselves

Human beings want to be seen, heard, and understood. Regardless of the title, position, or salary. This is the foundational basis of Compassionate Management – giving someone the gift of truly being Seen, Heard, and Understood. Most of this book has focused on you giving someone else the gift of being seen, heard, and understood. Now it's your turn.

The truth is this: No one cares more about your career than you, nor should they.

It's our responsibility to ensure that we get what we need and what we want out of our careers. So let's use Compassionate Management to help us follow our inner compass to get there.

Managing Up, Down, and Across

Managing people is something we do all day long. If a drugstore salesperson is grumpy, you smile and say, "How're you doing; rough day?" and after he says "Oh, hanging in there," you ask for help with getting the tissues you can't reach and he hands them to you with a smile. You've gotten what you needed by letting him feel listened to and understood. You managed him with compassion and that made him receptive to giving you what you needed.

Everybody wants to be seen, heard and understood, and I can understand why. Frankly, I'll do more for someone who makes me feel this way, and I know it works with those around me. It's a give/give relationship. I show you respect, you show it back.

In the drugstore, there's no history between you and the salesperson, so your management is pure, clean, and spontaneous. In other words, you trust your instinct to guide your approach. It's instinctive to be compassionate. Even if we are managed with fear for years and years, once we tap into our innate compassionate nature, it comes quite easily.

We are instinctively compassionate managers, if we just trust our instincts to guide us.

Being a manager requires working closely with human beings and holding them accountable to deliver the goods. This can be scary for people who have been promoted due to their talent, yet given no management training. Does that sound familiar to you? That's most managers. For most of us, we get caught on the "I don't know what I don't know" wheel of fear and that clouds our judgment. We get caught up in wanting people to like us. That is the kiss of you-know-what for leadership.

Focus on gaining respect rather than trying to have everyone like you.

Most people prefer to know where they stand with their boss. What's due when, how to improve their performance and what's their next step. Compassionate management includes being direct with kindness. There's no need to dance around something if it's facts communicated with respect.

> Example: I was promoted to manager. With no training whatsoever, I dove in to manage my friends, my drinking buddies. I quietly whispered "please, could you, when you can, do the report we talked about, but, whenever you can," even though I needed to deliver it right away.
>
> I quickly learned that it was annoying to my team that I was meekly managing them. They wanted, needed, leadership and clear priorities. Yes, they were annoyed that I had been their peer and was now their supervisor, but then I might as well get on with it and do it. It took me a long time to figure out that treating people with respect is what matters to them. I fell on my face so many times and just kept getting up. Moving from peer to manager is the hardest transition in

a career. Rather quickly I realized that I was no longer invited to drinks on a regular basis. It was sad, and appropriate.

We can't please all the people all the time, but we can always be respectful.

Think about your boss. Does he drive you crazy with apologetic suggestions or does he communicate in straightforward, compassionately stated requests? I'll take window number 2 any day.

Start watching people you believe are good managers and learn how they manage you and others around you.

Take note of when you feel listened to and when you don't. (This is listening to your instinct.)

Then try out different styles to develop your own version of managing compassionately; note any changes - or not - when you're managing your boss (up), your direct reports (down), or your colleagues (across).

Work to hone your ability to recognize when it's instinct guiding you or you're dancing around someone's personal situation. Most often, a straightforward and compassionate approach is more kind and more effective than getting tangled and inarticulate because of someone's personal situation. Compassionate management is that balance of business and heart.

Getting Promoted

I asked my boss what I needed to do to be promoted and she said I needed to move from a pure tactical to a more strategic role. What the heck does that mean? I'll tell you.

What she was telling me was to shift how I look at resolving problems and issues; to move from sitting in the details to looking at the bigger picture.

This shift is the key to getting promoted and being seen as a leader. It means coming up with ideas that answer logistical needs as well as have a positive financial impact for the company.

It took a long time for me to figure that out. There was a lot of trial and error and once I figured it out, I wanted to shout it to the world. Please allow me to do this right now, with Legos.

Tactical: "In the weeds" is a common phrase for this sort of thinking. It's the tangible, often physical, steps taken to get something done. It's sorting the Legos into piles of color and shapes. Then, following the blueprint and building the Lego house according to the blueprint.

Strategic: "High level" is the phrase used for this kind of thinking. It's the concept of creating the Lego house, the reason for the house, the benefits of the house, and consideration of cost and time it will take to build the Lego house.

A manager, who wants to be seen as a leader, and get promoted, needs to be both tactical and strategic. This is the shift. We start out quite tactical and as we learn the dynamics of a company, the product, and the people over time, we can begin to understand the why and how of decisions made at the top. That's called context and it is essential for people who want to climb the ladder.

There's no way to make the shift from tactical to strategic without understanding the context in which we make this shift.

Why senior management funded certain projects, cancelled others, and promoted her over him are all clues to understanding the context in which we need to position ourselves for a promotion.

An actual example (no Legos here):

Problem: You work for a retail company and there is a room filled with 3,000 samples- shirts, pants, shoes. There are four departments sharing these samples, so it's a mess. People are repeatedly fighting over samples and losing them. It slows down productivity and creates an environment of frustration and distrust.

Solution 1: You suggest a plan of organizing the products on hangers and shelves so people can find the product they need, when they need it. That's a tactical solution.

Solution 2: Then you propose a library card system where everyone can check out the samples they need and the database will show the record of it. This database provides analyses of who used what when, what samples haven't been used in 4 weeks, and what samples were never used at all. This analysis would result in buying less of one sample next year, more of another, and clearing out the unused samples for a sample sale at the end of each season. That is strategic.

In other words, solving a day-to-day tactical challenge within your department is meeting expectations. Solving a company-wide challenge, reducing expenses, and possibly increasing revenue is exceeding expectations.

A strategic solution sets you apart from your peers and will likely get you promoted.

It's important to understand that this solution would not have been proposed without context – an understanding of why there were so many samples to begin with, who used them and why, what the challenges were, what the benefits were for changing the system, and what cost savings might be delivered as a result of the change in the system.

In fact, the company invested over $300,000 to implement this library system, which ended up saving them millions in samples and expedited productivity enormously. It also eliminated the steady fighting and created an environment of trust.

Another important fact- it took this manager two years to get this project approved. She was diplomatically tenacious about it, as she believed deep in her heart that it would benefit the entire company.

Yes, she got promoted! But if the idea you've delivered doesn't get you promoted, it's a great example for your next job interview.

Corporate Speak

"Throw it over the wall."

"Will do."

That was a typical conversation at company where I consulted some years ago. In the first few weeks, I tried to play along. I figured context might help me figure out what the heck they were saying. After two weeks of this, I finally asked for an explanation of "over the wall." Apparently it meant to share the information with another department, which department depended on the content. Not rocket science, but definitely not obvious.

I find corporate speak confusing, misleading, distracting, and condescending. And I've been known to use it with fervor.

Corporate Speak is a tool to help us feel included in the team, like a secret handshake.

Speaking others' language puts them at ease. When in Paris speak French, when in Holland speak Dutch. It's the compassionate thing to do and frankly, sometimes you need to play the game. I've used "navigate" to refer to relationships, project management databases, sailing, and office politics. Depending on the audience, I'll acknowledge how foreign the word or phrase felt on my tongue; this makes me more human and can work to my benefit. Again, depending on the audience.

Learn the corporate speak in your office, make a terminology sheet if you have to, and use it carefully and appropriately. I've gone to more than one mentor to ask about a phrase or word - "everyone keeps talking about 'over the wall.' What the heck is this and how and when do I use it?"

Corporate speak often includes acronyms. A lot of acronyms. Ask if someone has made an acronym cheat sheet. I bet it exists. Everyone finds them confusing and no one wants to look like a dope. Once you have the sheet, imagine how you'll have expedited the learning curve for new employees or consultants. Now that's a tactical and strategic solution! It also levels the playing field of who knows what definitions and who doesn't.

One way to make this sheet the most fun, and without calling anyone out for not knowing something, is to make it an anonymous game for the team. People start adding and one person can be the reviewer; chances are it'll be the longest-standing employee who knows the true definitions.

If you find corporate speak as nauseating as I sometimes do, take a deep breath and use it with a sense of humor. Like all challenges at work, you can fight it or embrace it and make it work for you.

No One Can Succeed Alone

Think about all the athletes and musicians you love. Imagine if they had to do everything on their own. No mentor, teacher, coach, teammate. I can't imagine it because it's not possible.

No one can succeed alone. Not even someone as amazing as you. The only question is, what kind of support is best suited for you right now?

There are two kinds of support in the work world: a partner in the shared situation and outside help. We like to think that our boss can be our partner, but there's a danger of being seen as weak if we ask our boss for too much guidance, brainstorming, and discussion. This is why it's important to have more than one source for guidance.

Asking for help is a sign of strength. It means that you're secure enough to know when you need support to do something right. A Compassionate Manager will recognize this and embrace those people who have the confidence to seek support. At the same time, if your boss is insecure, I recommend you keep this on the down low. And keep it completely confidential if this is not applauded in your culture. It doesn't need to be broadcast, but we all need these relationships.

We all need at least one person from whom we receive compassion and support, without being labeled a basket case.

Many people hire a business coach outside of the office to help them confidentially; others reach out to colleagues and friends. Most people have a combination of outside sounding boards and internal partners. A support network is not a formal entity, but more like a list of people in your head who you know you can go to for certain guidance. They can be in your department, in another department, or outside the office. Identify for yourself what you trust them to help you with- to vent, to advise, what kind of experience they have, whether they have good judgment in general- and keep this bank of support in your back pocket for when you need it.

They don't need to know they're part of a personal support group. You know it and that can be comforting and enable you to handle tough situations. Trust your gut when building your support network. It's a process of finding the right people and sometimes we make a mistake. That's okay, keep going.

If your organization has an official mentoring program, that's great. Please know that just because someone signed up to be a mentor doesn't mean they're trustworthy. It could be a life-changing and wonderful mentoring relationship or a false promise that backfires. Keep your radar on and trust your gut!

With Each Age Come Gifts

Whatever age you are, it's natural to wish you were a different one. More experienced, less jaded, more this, less that. What a waste of energy.

Be present and embrace where you are in your career, whatever your age.

The gift of being 21 is different from the gift of being 34, 46, 59, 68, or 77. Each age has its bonuses and challenges. The challenges are named all day long in your head; it's the bonuses we forget to call out. Name the bonuses out loud, write them down, and you'll feel the shift toward loving right where you are. I'll start the bonus list:

In our youth we bring:

    Excitement

    Fresh eyes

    No context in which to limit our thinking

    What else would you add?

As we age we learn:

    Compassion

    Patience

    Tolerance

    Ability to laugh at oneself

Compassionate Managers are aware of the instinct to judge ourselves because of age. We do it with full awareness until we decide to stop. It's no fun any way you slice it and it's definitely not productive.

Refuse to belittle yourself for your lack of experience or your old-fashioned ways. Take steps to help others recognize the gifts you bring, at whatever age you're at. Point out the benefit of that fresh viewpoint or that seasoned one, create a department list of bonuses across the ages, set up mentorship across the ages where the expectation is mutual mentoring- the new by the seasoned and the seasoned by the new. Collaborate across the years and see what comes up with this open and welcoming approach to age differences.

Recognizing the gifts of our age sets an expectation of how someone can treat us, including how we treat ourselves.

As we've discussed many times in this book, we can fight What Is or we can embrace it and work it for all it's worth. Every person has gifts. A manager's responsibility is to seek that gift and enable it to flourish in the best interest of the company. Age and what we know as it relates to our age is a gift. It's a matter of perception and that's completely within our control.

PDC Communication

We were at an offsite meeting discussing how to help our two departments partner with each other. There had been an increase in animosity, and a decrease in productivity as a result. Suddenly, a participant from the other department stood up and announced that she thought our department could streamline our processes and eliminate some roles, thereby moving the funds to increase her team.

Everyone froze as she spoke. We all were thinking, "How dare she suggest firing our people just to add more people to her team!" and "Who does she think she is! She's the one with no system in place!" The angry thoughts were like cartoon bubbles over our heads. Her manager looked around the room and quickly realized she had to put a stop to this immediately. She firmly said, "Let's take this offline." We all began breathing again, but we were left with the feeling that we couldn't trust our peer.

Was she wrong to share her idea? Regardless of level, title, or functional role, we are expected to contribute to the well-being of the company. Therefore it stands to reason that our ideas and insights are valuable. In fact, I'd go so far as to say it's imperative that we share our ideas. If we don't, we're just a pair of hands doing tactical tasks. But it's how we communicate our ideas that makes all the difference.

Sharing ideas carelessly can ruin a reputation and likely have ramifications we never considered possible.

Some people demand attention by force. They demand to be heard in such a way that it backfires. In the example above, she shouted her idea at us. We felt shut down and disregarded. We lost respect for her. Instead of forcing her idea on the entire room, she could have chosen a more appropriate approach. It's a choice to present ourselves as professionals who consider the ramifications of what we say. That's what PDC is all about. It's three words that guide us how to communicate most effectively:

Privately.

Diplomatically.

Compassionately.

Private, diplomatic, and compassionate communication style is an attitude above all else.

It's taking into consideration your colleagues' experience, agenda, and objectives and then redefining the problem and solution. It's a tone of voice for the ideas you're presenting. PDC is a tool to help us be conscious of how we present ourselves.

Privately:

Consider who will be affected by what you're sharing. One persons' "amazing" idea can inadvertently have huge repercussions such as job eliminations, so consider the audience.

Diplomatically:

State the facts of what you see as a challenge and state the facts of what you propose as a solution. Stay away from pronouns and personalization and emotion. And use diplomatic tenacity – the art of knowing when to stop!

Compassionately:

Recognize the challenges faced by all and catch yourself if you go down the path of righteousness. People are equally fallible and need compassion and understanding, no matter how frustrating the situation.

Everyone is worthy of being listened to. Take your place. It's better to go for it and fail than to be a wallflower and hide. This is part of your growth process and can be learned and mastered at any age.

Addendum: In fact, her proposal was valid. When we considered roles, responsibilities, and workload, we ultimately agreed to make the changes she had suggested. It was painful, but it was appropriate. But we never got over how our peer addressed a delicate situation with such lack of consideration and respect.

conclusion

Compassionate Management is a management style that helps us stay true to our innate kindness, our natural desire to succeed and thrive, our instinctive love of money and all it can offer us, and our basic human need for connection. In other words, all of this information is in your DNA, waiting for your attention. This book is simply a key to opening up to what you already know in your deepest knowing. Use this book when you start to feel your integrity slipping, your patience wearing thin, and your frustrations taking control. It'll help you tap back into You.

You've got the power.

10 Innate Tools of Compassionate Management

1. **Be Your Self**
   When we show up fully and quietly confident

2. **Trust Your Gut**
   When we trust our deepest knowing

3. **Own Your Power**
   When we control how we respond

4. **BOD, Baby**
   Giving others the Benefit of the Doubt

5. **Not Taking It Personally**
   When we decide it's not about us

6. **Coexisting Truths**
   Opposing truths do not negate each other

7. **Seen, Heard, and Understood**
   The universal desire

8. **Tone Of Voice**
   Meaning changes as our intonation changes

9. **Meet Your Inner Critic**
   Disarm the internal terrorist

10. **Be Self Aware**
    We choose who we want to be in this world

Management for Millennials

©2016 Management For Millennials | Follow @mgmtformill

about the author

Rena DeLevie is the Chief Compassion Officer of Management For Millennials, a business dedicated to replacing fear in the workplace with compassion and accountability. She is the author of *NTiP The 4-Step Formula For Not Taking It Personally*, a Huffington Post columnist, and a TEDx presenter, "Using Compassion As A Business Tool."

Ms. DeLevie created Compassionate Management, the leadership methodology, based on what she wished she had experienced in her career as an art director, designer, and creative operations executive in the creative sector. Her experiences with 9/11 woke her out of a fear-based trance and led to her realization that compassion was an innate and effective business tool. She began to practice compassion and accountability with her colleagues and saw immediate changes in how they reacted; there was collaboration, laughter, and trust.

With Compassionate Management, Ms. DeLevie combines her learnings from 30 years with Fortune 500 companies and 14 years as a practitioner of mindfulness and mindfulness meditation to show us the path to eliminate the fear-based culture so prevalent in corporate America. Through her presentations, workshops, and individual coaching, Ms. DeLevie is steadily empowering managers at every level to implement this new approach to leadership that is effective, efficient, and fun.

Ms. DeLevie's empathetic and business-focused approach has led to her being given a few nicknames including, "Hippie MBA," "COO of the Creative Process," "The Vault," and "How may I help you?"

Watch her TEDxTalk: "Using Compassion As A Business Tool"

Read her management column in Huffington Post: huffpost/renadelevie.

Email her: rena@managementformillennials.com

Learn more: www.managementformillennials.com.

books

I love reading and learning from others. I've chosen 22 of my favorites books from both business and Buddhist/mindfulness categories. Sometimes they cross over, like this book in your hands; sometimes they don't. It would be impossible to include every book that has had an impact on my work, my writing, and me, as I'm a voracious reader. Many novels have left a lasting impression as much as the non-fiction books listed below. I hope you find this list helpful.

The 100 Simple Secrets Of Successful People, What Scientists Have Learned And How You Can Use It, David Niven, Ph.D., Harper Collins, 2002
I needed a lite book to cheer me up about my job many years ago. I don't remember how I came across this one, but I'm grateful. It's quick, fun, and substantial. It helps me to this day when I need something uplifting and real.

A Whole New Mind, Why Right Brainers Will Rule The Future, Daniel H. Pink, The Penguin Group, 2005
I was considered a freak for being 50% right- and 50% left-brained for most of my career. Now it's trendy. This book made me feel seen, understood, and valuable. I was giddy and squealing, "Yes!" as I read each page. Thank you Mr. Pink.

Breaking The Timer Barrier, How To Unlock Your True Earning Potential, Mike McDermott and Donald Cowper, FreshBooks, 2013

Written by the CEO of FreshBooks, an accounting solution for small businesses, this tiny book is a powerful and quick read. It will show you your value without getting into salary ranges or other boring details. It's a story that I have shared with many clients and it has changed all of our lives for the better.

The Circle of Innovation, You Cant Shrink Your Way To Greatness, Tom Peters, Vintage Books, 1997
What fun this book is! It has pictures and drawings and huge words and tiny words. The words are meaningful and demystifying. This book showed me that a management book can be fun.

The Diamond Cutter, The Buddha on Managing Your Business and Your Life, Geshe Michael Roach, Doubleday, 2000
It's a deep book that helped me connect my spiritual path with my love of business. When you want to go deep, go here.

Feel The Fear And Do It Anyway, Dynamic techniques for turning fear, indecision, and anger into power, action, and love, Susan Jeffers, Ph.D., Ballantine Books, 1987, 2007
It works. Read this when you're feeling frozen with fear and it'll kick you in the pants in just the right way.

The Five Dysfunctions Of A Team, A Leadership Fable, Patrick Lencioni, Jossey-Bass, 2002
A classic fable that illustrates true leadership through example made it easy to understand the concept of leadership when I was but a newbie, and fun to read. I still have post it notes in the book.

Healing The Corporate World, How Values-Based Leadership Transforms Business From The Inside Out, Maria Gamb, 2010
Maria gets it. She speaks spiritual and business and bottom line in each sentence. This book showed me that there is a community of like-minded leaders and helped me find my individual path.

Inviting a Monkey To Tea, Befriending Your Mind and Discovering Lasting Contentment, Nancy Colier, Hohm Press, 2012
I will read anything Ms. Colier writes because she writes in a language that resonates for me. This book helped me understand the role anxiety plays in our lives and empowered me to help my clients, and myself.

Just Blow It Up, Firepower For Living An Unlimited Life, Dixie Gillaspie, Sound Wisdom, 2012
Dixie is a powerhouse who dives straight to the core of the issue. She is dynamic, authentic, and connected to her deepest knowing, which helps me connect to mine.

Lovingkindness: The Revolutionary Art of Happiness, Sharon Salzberg, Shambhala Classics, September 3, 2002
An easy, serious, and fun read that explained LovingKindness, a Buddhist approach to life, in a way that I could relate to as a layperson.

Liquid Leadership: From Woodstock to Wikipedia--Multigenerational Management Ideas That Are Changing the Way We Run Things by Brad Szollose Greenleaf Book Group Press

This book articulates what you feel at work everyday - how the old order is no more and what the new order could be. It's an articulate, fun, and powerful read. Brad was my co-TEDx speaker and he does an incredible Christopher Walken impersonation.

Managing Oneself, Peter Drucker, Harvard Business Review Classics, 1995, 2005, 2008

The content of this book is classic Drucker. He gets to the point in language that is accessible from entry level to C-Suite. The format makes me happy. It's a concise handbook that gave me permission to write the way I wanted, not the way I thought I should write.

Nonviolent Communication, A Language of Life, Marshall B. Rosenberg, Ph.D., PuddleDancer Press 2003

This book title sounds alarming, but NVC is a loving and compassionate way to communicate. This book positively changed how I communicate with my friends, loved ones, and colleagues. There is a parenting version that I keep in my night table; *Raising Children Compassionately, Parenting the Nonviolent Communication Way* also by Marshall B. Rosenberg, Ph.D.

The Only Dance There Is, Talks at the Menninger Foundation 1970 and Spring Grive Hospital 1972, Ram Dass, Anchor Books, 1974

Who doesn't want to climb inside Ram Dass's head? I did. And I enjoyed the ride. This was a groovy, funky, and spacious journey into Buddhism and real life. If that resonates for you, pick up a copy.

Purple Cow Transform Your business By Being Remarkable, Seth Godin PORTFOLIO Penguin Group, 2003
Each word is purposeful, meaningful, and cuts to the core of what Mr. Godin is teaching. This book shifted my thinking from trying to fit in to allowing myself to stand out. It's terrifying and empowering.

Radical Acceptance: Embracing Your Life With the Heart of a Buddha, Tara Brach, Bantam– November 23, 2004
This book changed my relationship with myself. It's one of the few books I've read more than once. This stays with me in times of discord and keeps me centered and clear about who I am and who I want to be in this world. Me.

Rework, Jason Fried & David Heinemeier Hansson, Crown Business, 2010
I loved the balance of technology, heart, business, and fun. I flew threw this book and absorbed the multiple lessons that came through the serious and funny anecdotes and stories shared. It showed me that you can be serious and funny simultaneously in a business book.

Who Moved My Cheese, An A-Mazing Way To Deal With Change In Your Work and in Your Life, Spencer Johnson, M.D., Penguin Putnam, 1998

A small book with a huge message that resonates with me to this day. I give this as gifts and teach the message repeatedly: that change is hard for everyone, but less so for those who are prepared.

Working with Emotional Intelligence, Daniel Goleman, Bantam, 1998

I pretty much hugged Mr. Goleman when I met him recently. This book made it safe for me to be me. It said so many things I thought were unacceptable at work because all I knew was fear-based management. He's a nice person, too.

The Wise Heart, A Guide To The Universal Teachings of Buddhist Psychology, Jack Kornfield, Bantam, 2008

I've heard Jack Kornfield speak at multiple events and have had side conversations with him. A gentle being, he writes and teaches Buddhist Psychology in language that made me question if I wanted to switch to psychology as a career. It's not light reading; it's academic in an accessible language.

Your Network Is Your Net Worth: Unlock the Hidden Power of Connections for Wealth, Success, and Happiness in the Digital Age by Porter Gale, Atria Books

It's about community, not forced conversation. I stand by this idea - it works for me over and over - and Porter happens to be a genuinely nice person.

acknowledgements

I want to thank my family for standing by me even when you didn't understand what I was doing. To my father Ari, you inspire me with your kindness, creativity, and courage. To my sisters, Sharon and Tammy - we get through anything together. I thank God for you both. To my mother Joan, you were irreverent, funny, and whip-smart. I wish you were here to enjoy this with me. To my Grams, I imagine you'd be squealing with nachus at this book and at all I've accomplished since you passed away. I carry you with me. To Dietmar and Steven – I am so lucky to have such great brothers in law. To Rachel, Sophia, Eliana, Jessie, Jeremy and Julia - thank you for laughing with me and sometimes at me. To my cuzisters, Julie and Wendy, my Fraunt Diane, Aya, all my aunts, uncles, cousins, nieces, and nephews, and to my chosen family Cookie, Florie, and Joey – I am grateful for you. We are blessed, we are blessed, we are blessed.

I have had incredible mentors. To Nancy Colier, thank you for being my therapist, my Buddhist guide, my meditation teacher, and my mentor. Because of your endless compassion, I've been able to show up and live the life I was meant to lead instead of squeezing myself into others ideas of me. To Maria Gamb, thank you for being my friend in college all those years ago and for re-entering my life at just the right time. Without you, this book would never have been completed. To Dixie Gillaspie, thank you for your courage, intensity, and ability to take what is felt in our deepest heart and put it in written form. To Anne Secor, you win the award for patience and outstanding client management. And of course great design! Your support while designing this book has been a source of comfort to me and kept me going when I wanted to crawl into bed.

Community and friendship is crucial to my happiness. To my friends who believe in me, I say thank you. Stephanie and Adam, Helen, Palma, Chris and Lee, Ellen, Lana, Joanie, Anna, and Ken. I wouldn't have had the courage to let my voice be heard without your support. I want to thank my synagogue, Romemu, for the space to Be. When I sing with my synagogue community of people of all races, religions, gender, sexuality, and age, I feel a connection to my deepest knowing that we, all people, are equal and loved.

And to the hundreds of colleagues I interacted with over the years who cheered me on or guided me to evolve overtly or subtly, I appreciate you. To Lori Wagner, Rachel Cusak, Christina Schoonmaker, Jaimee Given, Amy Rasner, and especially Paul Coviello, who carried me through one of the darkest periods of my working life.

To my clients. Thank you for trusting me to guide you to your greatest self. I learn from you every day and I'm grateful to be of service to you.

And to my son Oren, my miracle and my blessing. You bring me the greatest joy imaginable. Your smile lights up my heart and makes me know how deep my love can go. One look, text, or word from you, one glance at you, and I know gratitude, deeply and truly. I love you.

working with rena

Read below and then email rena@managementformillennials.com to learn more.

Private Individual Coaching: Rena works with people who are serious about evolving the way they interact with colleagues of any level. This is for creative leaders, creatives who want to be leaders, non-creatives who want to understand their colleagues, and creative entrepreneurs who want to cut through the chatter and define their path.

Corporate Cross-Coaching: Bring Rena in to work with one or multiple departments. Rena will work with 6 people individually, one day a week. This cross-coaching lowers walls, builds trust, and expedites communication. The seats are open to any who choose to sign up - across function, tenure, gender, generation, ethnicity, sexuality, religion – as well as those who are confidentially required to receive management training. This coaching structure enables those required to learn without an audience, and gives leadership the opportunity to discover who has undiscovered potential.

Seminars and Workshops: There's nothing like raucous laughter to help people internalize a new approach to management and partnership. In an experiential and interactive setting, attendees are invited to discuss real-life situations and experience how compassion & accountability can be used to clarify, expedite, and deliver great results. Topics include these top 4 requested presentations:

1. Not Taking It Personally - Attendees learn the formula for Not Taking It Personally and how to implement it with effective and diplomatic results, even when furious.

2. Managing Up, Down, and Across - The mindset of management is seeded. Scripts are created by the attendees, and become default language for managing senior leadership, peers, and direct reports successfully.

3. Communicating Effectively - Awareness of how tone of voice, body language and content can affect us, and others, and the ways in which we can manage our communication most effectively.

4. The Path to a Seat at the Leadership Table - Attendees learn the tools with which to perform at a higher level.

Corporate Events: Offsite team building days, conferences, retreats, lunch and learn; there are many ways Rena has helped leaders bring about change. She makes it fun, engaging and accessible. She works with leadership to determine the best approach to accomplishing the goals of the event and then customizes materials to deliver.

Webinars: Watch from home, the office or on the plane; live or recorded. Webinars can be custom topics or chosen from the Management For Millennials library.

Contact

Management for Millennials

managementformillennials.com
rena@managementformillennials.com
@mgmtformill